Essential Rational Emotive Behaviour Therapy

MICHAEL NEENAN

Centre for Stress Management, London

AND

WINDY DRYDEN

Goldsmiths College, University of London

W

WHURR PUBLISHERS

LONDON AND PHILADELPHIA

© 2000 Whurr Publishers
First published 2000 by
Whurr Publishers Ltd
19b Compton Terrace, London N1 2UN, England and
325 Chestnut Street, Philadelphia PA 19106, USA

British Library Cataloguing in Publication Data
A catalogue record for this book is available from the
British Library.

ISBN: 1 86156 160 1

Printed and bound in the UK by Athenaeum Press Ltd,
Gateshead, Tyne & Wear

Contents

Preface

Since the inception of rational emotive behaviour therapy (REBT) in 1955, its theory and practice have been expanded, corrected, updated and revised (Bard, 1980; Dryden, 1991a; Ellis, 1994; Ellis and Dryden, 1997; Grieger and Boyd, 1980; Neenan and Dryden, 1999; Wessler and Wessler, 1980). Much of this inevitable modification has focused upon the ABCDE model of emotional disturbance and change, the centrepiece of REBT theory and practice. While the model still appears to be relatively simple to explain to clients and trainee REBTers, in other ways 'the ABCs of rational-emotive therapy ... are exceptionally interactional and therefore in many ways complex' (Ellis, 1985a, 1991, 1993). We have added to this complexity by breaking down the model into a 13-step counselling sequence (Dryden and DiGiuseppe, 1990) and, more recently, increasing the number of steps to 18 (Dryden, Neenan and Yankura, 1999).

While some REB therapists might praise these innovations, others make criticisms along the lines of 'you're making it too complicated for most clients to understand and probably some REBTers too!'. Innovations are the lifeblood of any therapy that wishes to remain dynamic but, obviously, not everyone involved with or interested in REBT cares about or can keep up with such developments. From their perspective, an understanding of basic theory and a reasonable level of competent practice is sufficient. So with this in mind, we have decided to strip away the sophistication and focus on the essential elements of REBT written, we hope, in an easy-to-read style. Such a challenge reminds us that keeping it simple in REBT can be the hardest task of all.

Chapter 1
An Outline of REBT

In this chapter, we discuss key features of REBT theory and practice which include the ABCDE model of emotional disturbance and change, rigid and extreme beliefs which we contrast with flexible and non-extreme beliefs, ego and discomfort disturbance, unhealthy and healthy negative emotions, active-directiveness as a counsellor, and elegant and inelegant change.

Introduction

Rational emotive behaviour therapy (REBT) is a system of psychotherapy which teaches individuals how their belief systems are mainly responsible for the way they feel about and act towards events in their lives. Events contribute to our emotional problems but do not cause them. Emotional and behavioural change in REBT comes from identifying, challenging and changing those beliefs which largely create our emotional problems. REBT was founded in 1955 by Albert Ellis, an American psychologist, and was a pioneering form of cognitive-behaviour therapy and remains a leading approach within the cognitive-behavioural movement.

The ABCDE model of emotional disturbance and change

This model is at the heart of REBT theory and practice. Every problem is placed within this framework in order to teach the client and guide the therapist. In the model:

A = activating event. This refers to what actually happened or an inference of what happened. Activating events can be past, present or future and experienced internally or externally.

iB = irrational beliefs. These beliefs are called irrational because they evaluate the activating event in a rigid and extreme way.

C = emotional and behavioural consequences. These unhealthy negative emotions and self-defeating behaviours are largely determined by our irrational beliefs about these events.

D = disputing. This involves challenging or questioning the irrational beliefs at B that produce our emotional and behavioural reactions at C.

E = a new and effective rational outlook. This is achieved through the disputing process and the constructive behaviour that results from it.

It is vital you teach clients that B, not A, largely determines C otherwise your clients will see changing events at A rather than disputing at D as the solution to their problems.

Rigid and extreme beliefs

REBT states that rigid and absolute beliefs are to be found at the core of our emotional disturbance. These beliefs usually come in the form of musts, shoulds, oughts, have to's and got to's, e.g. 'I must always be liked otherwise I'm no good.' Such a belief is likely to produce, for example, hurt or depression when the individual is told that he is unlikeable. It is important to point out that REBT's focus is usually on challenging and changing *unconditional* musts and shoulds rather than conditional ones, e.g. 'I must never show any weaknesses' v. 'I must get a move on if I want to get to the cinema on time' respectively. The unconditional must is more likely to create serious emotional disturbance than the conditional one if the must is not met. Listening for the meaning behind musts and shoulds is a very important skill in REBT if you are to avoid tackling needlessly every must or should uttered by your clients.

Flowing from these rigid musts and shoulds etc. are three major derivatives couched in an extreme form:

1. Awfulizing – this refers to defining negative events as so terrible that they seem incomprehensible when viewed against our everyday reality or experience, e.g. 'I just can't believe that so many bad things can happen to someone in the space of a week. It's awful.' Another way to view awfulizing is that our personal world has come to a horrible end because we refuse to accept the grim reality of events. Awfulizing also implies that no good can possibly come from the bad things that happen to us.

2. Low frustration tolerance (LFT) – this is the perceived inability to endure frustration or discomfort in our lives and to envisage any happiness while such conditions exist, e.g. 'I'm going to blow my top. I can't stand any more traffic jams'. LFT is also referred to as 'I can't-stand-it-

itis'. Walen, DiGiuseppe and Dryden (1992, p. 8) suggest that 'LFT is perhaps the main reason that clients do not improve after they have gained an understanding of their disturbance and how they create it.'

3. Depreciation of self, others and/or life conditions – this involves placing a global negative label on ourselves or others based on a particular action or trait, e.g. 'Because I failed my exam for the second time, I'm a useless person.' Rating ourselves on the basis of our behaviour is a habit that is often hard to break.

These rigid and extreme beliefs are called irrational (self-defeating) because they are illogical (i.e. do not make sense), unrealistic, block or interfere with us achieving our goals and lead to a good deal of emotional distress. These beliefs can be seen as demands or commands we make on *ourselves*, e.g. 'I must never show any weaknesses'; *others*, e.g. 'You must always treat me with respect'; or *the world/life*, e.g. 'Life musn't be too hard on me.' By forcefully and persistently disputing these demands and commands through a variety of methods and tasks, we can develop a problem-solving outlook that brings greater control over our lives.

Flexible and non-extreme beliefs

Flexible beliefs are based on wishes, wants, preferences, desires and are called rational (self-helping) because they are logical (i.e. make sense), realistic, aid goal-attainment and lead to healthy rather than unhealthy negative emotions. This means that we experience emotional discontent (a qualitative change) instead of emotional disturbance in the face of life's adversities, e.g. 'I hope that other people do like me but, unfortunately, they don't have to do so.' Instead of feeling hurt or depressed, the individual who holds these flexible beliefs will feel disappointed or sad about the reactions of others.

Flowing from these wishes and preferences etc. are three major derivatives couched in a non-extreme form and acting as constructive alternatives to the ones described above:

1. Anti-awfulizing – negative events are viewed along a scale of badness that can be comprehended within our everyday reality and experience once these events are accepted as having occurred, e.g. 'I never thought that so many bad things would happen to me so quickly. Things are bleak but not awful.' Our personal world may have been severely battered but not shattered or brought to an end. Anti-awfulizing also implies that some good can come from the bad things that happen to us.

2. Higher frustration tolerance (HFT) – learning to increase our ability to withstand discomfort and hardship in life and still enjoy some measure of stability or happiness, e.g. 'I certainly don't like being stuck in traffic jams but I can put up with them without blowing my top.' Acquiring HFT helps your clients to endure the effort involved in reaching their goals.

3. Acceptance of self, others and life conditions – human beings are seen as fallible (imperfect) and in a state of continuous change; therefore it is futile to give ourselves a single global rating as this can never fully describe or encompass the totality of what it means to be human, e.g. 'Even though I failed my exam for a second time, I refuse to condemn myself as worthless. I am too complex to be rated in any way.' We can choose to rate our actions or traits if this is deemed to be helpful in some way. Also, life conditions are seen as composed of a complex mixture of negative, positive and neutral events.

Hierarchical organization of thinking

As noted above, REBT sees irrational beliefs as the main determinant of emotional disturbance. Therefore not all of our cognitive activity or thinking is deemed to be as equally important in understanding our emotional difficulties. REBT suggests there are different levels of thinking that we need to be aware of in tackling these difficulties. As a rule of thumb, the deeper the level, the greater the degree of difficulty in uncovering and changing these cognitions:

Inferences – these are personally significant assumptions about events which may or may not be true. This type of thought is relatively easy to gain access to by asking, for example, 'What is going through your mind when you think about the party this weekend?' Reply: 'No-one is going to pay any attention to me.' Inferences are often linked and these can be revealed by asking 'Let's assume that's true, then what?' questions. This process is known as inference chaining and is an important pathway into deeper layers of clients' thinking. Inferences come under the 'A' heading in the ABC model.

Specific evaluative beliefs – these are specific appraisals of our inferences; in other words, we make up our minds about situations and deliver judgements. With regard to the above example, the individual declares: 'I must not be ignored at the party.' This is an example of a situation-specific evaluative belief. Evaluative beliefs are also held at a general level and cover a number of situations including parties: 'Other people must always show an interest in me.' These evaluative beliefs, particularly at the general level, may not be readily accessible to clients as they often remain unspoken. When evaluative beliefs are at the root of our emotional problems and encompass a broad range of situations, they are known as core beliefs.

Core beliefs – these are the central philosophies we use to understand ourselves, others and the world. Negative core beliefs (e.g. 'I'm a failure') can be very difficult to detect as they remain dormant during periods of stability in our lives. However, they usually become activated and pass into our awareness when we experience emotional distress or unpleasant events. Inference chaining of a number of situations in which we experience emotional problems can uncover such beliefs and help to make their content explicit.

We may well construct our core beliefs at earlier stages in our lives (e.g. childhood, adolescence) and they are often instrumental in shaping our worldview. When emotional disturbance has moderated, negative core beliefs become deactivated. Core beliefs can be seen as 'light sleepers' as they are often easily woken when we run into problems in our lives; with some individuals (e.g. personality disorders) these core beliefs are active a good deal of the time. A core belief from which the above inferences and evaluative beliefs ultimately derive could be: 'I must know that others like me otherwise this will prove I'm worthless.' Core beliefs are the ultimate target of REBT intervention if clients are to achieve what Ellis calls 'a profound philosophical change' in their outlook.

Two types of disturbance

REBT suggests that two types of emotional disturbance underlie most, if not all, neurotic problems: ego and discomfort. The former relates to demands made upon ourselves, others or the world and the resulting self-denigration when these demands are not met, e.g. 'As I didn't get the promotion, which I absolutely should have done, this means I'm an incompetent person.' The latter type involves demands made upon ourselves, others or the world that comfortable life conditions must exist and the consequent frustration when they do not, e.g. 'I absolutely shouldn't have lost my job. I can't stand all the hassle involved in looking for another one!'

Ego and discomfort disturbance are separate categories but frequently overlap in clients' presenting problems as when, for example, a man condemns himself as weak (ego) for being unable to cope with a high-pressure job (discomfort). In assessing clients' problems, you need to be alert to both the ego and discomfort aspects of these problems.

Hedonism: short- and long-term perspectives

Hedonism in REBT does not mean pursuing a life solely based on experiencing pleasure. Rather, REBT seeks to help individuals to achieve a balance between enjoying the pleasures of the present and working towards the achievement of future goals, e.g. going to parties at university as well as studying hard to pass exams and thereby increase job opportunities. Such a balance is seen as responsible hedonism. Encouraging clients who are primarily short-term thinkers (e.g. drug addicts) to develop longer-term thinking in order to tackle their problems successfully can be an exceedingly difficult task.

Two forms of responsibility

The first form is emotional responsibility whereby we accept that our emotional problems are largely created by our beliefs. The ABC model establishes emotional responsibility:

A = Being rejected by one's partner.
B = 'I'm nothing without her'.
C = Depression and withdrawal.

Being rejected is unfortunate but the depression is determined by the individual's evaluation of being rejected, not the act of rejection itself.

The second form is therapeutic responsibility whereby we commit ourselves to the hard work of personal change by disputing our disturbance-creating beliefs. The D and E elements of the model encourage therapeutic responsibility:

D = 'Even though rejection is painful, there is no reason why it must not happen to me. Others have the power to reject me but I have the power not to damn myself because of it and therefore will no longer do so.'
E = A new and effective outlook that decreases this person's fear of rejection and increases his or her opportunities for finding new partners.

If your clients want to achieve a successful outcome in REBT, then it is vital that they accept and act on both forms of responsibility.

Developing an emotional vocabulary

Dryden (1999a) suggests that emotional reactions to harsh or unpleasant life events can be divided into healthy and unhealthy negative emotions (see Table 1.1).

Table 1.1: Healthy and unhealthy negative emotions

Unhealthy	Healthy
Anxiety	Concern
Depression	Sadness
Guilt	Remorse
Shame	Disappointment
Hurt	Sorrow
Unhealthy anger (at person)	Healthy anger (only at person's behaviour)
Unhealthy jealousy (possessive)	Healthy jealousy (non-possessive protection of one's relationship)
Unhealthy envy (malicious)	Healthy envy (non-malicious desire to possess another's advantages or good fortune)

Demands and their extreme derivatives drive unhealthy negative emotions, e.g. the anxiety-inducing belief 'I must not fail at this task otherwise my life will be awful', while preferences and their non-extreme derivatives underlie healthy negative emotions, e.g. the concern-creating belief 'I certainly don't want to fail at this task but I'm not immune from doing so. If I do, my life will become much harder but not awful.'

This emotional vocabulary is not meant to be forced on to your clients but acts as a starting point for them to identify and discuss which emotions they want to tackle and how they would like to feel instead. Also, feeling unhealthy negative emotions is not wrong in any absolute sense: it is often the degree of disturbance that clients experience and the desire to modify it that is the focus of clinical attention.

Biologically-based tendencies

Ellis (1976) argues that we have two powerful inborn tendencies to think both irrationally and rationally about events in our lives. Our biological predisposition to think irrationally does not mean that we will continually disturb ourselves throughout life: a tendency is not an inevitability. Therefore this tendency towards irrational thinking can be checked (but probably not removed) by our other innate tendency towards rational thinking, i.e. to scrutinize our irrational ideas. Obviously some clients will blame their upbringing, environment etc. for their current problems and exclude any biological factors. In order to avoid drawn-out discussions or arguments over this issue, an assortment of factors can be acknowledged in the development of the problem and irrational ideas as the central means of maintaining it. The point is to deal with the emotional disturbance *now* rather than haggle over its source.

Postmodern perspective

A postmodern outlook is sceptical of universal theories or truths – philosophical, political, religious, cultural, scientific – which claim to explain the world and our place within it. The postmodern rejection of omniscience (being all-knowing) gives way to a relativist position on knowledge, truth, values and encourages a plurality of viewpoints. The postmodern mind should 'take nothing for granted, treat all as provisional, assume no absolutes' (Tarnas, 1996, p. 396).

REBT takes a postmodern stance as it rejects all absolutist thinking (e.g. rigid musts and shoulds) and therefore does not endorse any absolute truths. Ellis (Ellis and MacLaren, 1998) states that he is a moderate postmodernist and not a radical one, e.g. radical postmodernists would argue that reality is entirely self-constructed and there is no external reality to consider while REBT suggests that our individual realities are mediated by our inferences and evaluative beliefs which can then be subjected to testing to ascertain if they are congruent with empirical reality (e.g. does the world reflect an individual's demands that he must never make a mistake?).

The terms 'irrational' and 'rational' in REBT are used as relative constructs and not employed with any sense of absolute certainty or authority: what is irrational is determined by clients as blocking goal-attainment (e.g. unassertiveness) and what is rational is determined by clients as aiding goal-attainment (e.g. risk-taking). Ellis suggests that REBT has always been moderately postmodern (for further discussion of postmodernism and REBT see Ellis, 1997).

Maintenance of emotional disturbance

REBT focuses on how emotional problems are being maintained in the present through continual irrational thinking rather than on how these problems were acquired in the past. As discussed above, environmental factors play their part in the development of our problems but not in its continuation, e.g. a man believes he is unlovable because his parents showed him little affection as a child; instead of subjecting this belief to scrutiny when he got older, he continues to remind himself that he is unlovable. The historical perspective is not neglected in REBT but is best viewed through the lens of the present, e.g. 'You said that you are still angry today about your father's behaviour towards you thirty years ago. Shall we examine the beliefs that have been driving your anger for the last thirty years?'

Active-directive style

This is often a focused approach that actively guides clients to the salient aspects of their presenting problems and is deemed to be more effective in helping clients change than a passive or nondirective style of intervention. REBT therapists are active in, among other activities, asking questions, collecting assessment data, limiting extraneous material or client rambling, problem defining, goal-setting, teaching, disputing and negotiating homework tasks – all these and other activities are aimed at directing clients to the cognitive core (i.e. rigid and extreme musts and shoulds) of their emotional and behavioural problems. In order to get clients to this cognitive destination, Walen, DiGiuseppe and Dryden (1992, p. 229) 'envision the therapist as a kind of herd dog who guides the patient through an open field full of distractions, keeping the patient on course'.

Active-directiveness is the general style of REBTers but it will need to be adjusted to meet the preferences (e.g. a slow pace), learning requirements (e.g. repetition of key REBT points) and interpersonal functioning (e.g. a subdued approach with a histrionic client) of individual clients. If you assume that active-directive always means highly active and overly directive this can have an adverse impact on some of your clients by minimizing their self-responsibility for change, impairing their problem-solving abilities and undermining the development of a collaborative relationship.

Elegant and inelegant change

Ellis (1993) argues that, ideally, REBT should (preferably) be helping clients to achieve an elegant solution to their problems, i.e. removing rigid and absolute musts, shoulds and their extreme derivatives from their thinking in order to reduce present and future emotional disturbance. This is largely achieved by encouraging clients to assume the worst about their problems or reality and learning to cope with it without undue emotional disturbance. With less disturbance to contend with, clients have a better chance of achieving self-actualization (i.e. realizing their potential). If humans can rid themselves of their rigid musts and shoulds (as far as is humanly possible), Ellis argues we can then make ourselves less disturbable but not undisturbable. The elegant solution is also called achieving a profound philosophical change.

However, some clients, perhaps many, may find that achieving the elegant solution is beyond their capability or interest. In these cases, REBT offers an inelegant solution, i.e. providing symptom relief and limited generalizability to other problems in their lives. For example, clients can challenge and change their distorted inferences (assumptions) about events rather than the underlying irrational beliefs that give rise to these inferences; so when a man suspects his wife of unfaithfulness he is shown that the evidence does not confirm his suspicions instead of encouraging him to dispute his belief that 'My wife must not be unfaithful and if she is, this will prove how utterly undesirable I am.'

Other inelegant solutions are changing unpleasant activating events rather than confronting them (e.g. looking for another job rather than dealing with difficulties with colleagues) and behaviourally-based change (e.g. entering previously avoided situations but still holding the irrational belief 'It would be awful if no one came and spoke to me'). In essence, the inelegant solution is not accompanied by philosophical change. It is important that you do not indicate to your clients that the inelegant solution is an inferior outcome (how do you know what impact it will have on their lives?). Remember that theoretical predictions can and do prove false in practice.

Helping clients to get better and not just feel better

Ellis (1972) says this is one of the key factors in REBT. Clients will come to see you to help them effect an amelioration of their presenting problems (e.g. anxiety, depression, substance abuse, high stress levels). This can be achieved by, among other ways, teaching relaxation techniques, ventilating feelings, providing warmth and reassurance, prescribing drugs. While some, even many, clients will say they feel better after a few sessions with you, REBT hypothesizes that these clients will not actually get and stay better because they have not yet uncovered, challenged and changed their key disturbance-producing philosophies. For example, a woman who has been rejected by her friends and becomes depressed believes 'I must be liked by others in order to prove I'm not worthless.' Instead of challenging this philosophy and replacing it with unconditional self-acceptance, the therapist tells her that she is worthwhile, thereby reinforcing conditional self-acceptance. The client leaves therapy feeling better but relapses into depression several weeks later when a new friendship founders. It is very important that you teach your clients the differences between feeling and getting better; this can encourage them to work longer and harder in therapy in order to achieve the latter goal.

Relapse prevention or reduction

These strategies teach clients how to reduce or remove future episodes of emotional disturbance. This involves persistently and forcefully strengthening emerging rational (flexible and non-extreme) beliefs and weakening long-standing disturbance-producing (rigid and extreme) beliefs. If clients do slide back into emotional disturbance, Ellis (1984) advises them to 'look for the must, look for the absolute should' that has entered into their thinking again. By using the ABCDE model, clients can quickly limit the damage that a relapse may cause. Relapse prevention strategies are usually built-in to the last few sessions of REBT.

Three REBT insights

REBT is an insight and action-orientated therapy because it provides clients with a clear understanding of the role of rigid and extreme thinking in their emotional problems and what remedial steps can be taken. In particular, REBT presents clients with three major insights into the development, maintenance and eventual improvement of their problems:

1. Human disturbance is largely determined by irrational beliefs. To paraphrase Epictetus, a Stoic philosopher from the first century AD: people are disturbed not by things, but by their rigid and extreme views of things.
2. We remain disturbed in the present because we continually re-indoctrinate or brainwash ourselves with these beliefs and act in ways that strengthen them.
3. The only enduring way to overcome our emotional problems is through persistent hard work and practice – to think, feel and act against our irrational beliefs.

These three insights provide clients with a capsule account of REBT and act as a lifelong guide to emotional and behavioural problem-solving.

In this chapter, we have provided an overview of REBT theory and practice. Armed with this information, the next step is to undertake an assessment of your clients' presenting problems which is the focus of the next chapter.

Chapter 2
Assessment

In this chapter, we look at the elements required to conduct a clinical assessment which includes asking for a problem, focusing on the aspect of the presenting problem which the client is most disturbed about, locating an unhealthy negative emotion and the irrational belief underpinning it, and agreeing on client goals for change.

Introduction to REBT

Most clients who seek therapy probably have no idea of the counselling orientation of the practitioner or may subscribe to some popular notions that therapy is all about exploring their childhood or blaming their parents for everything that is wrong in their present lives. You can deal with these issues by discussing clients' expectations of therapy along with any previous experiences of therapy. You can put clients 'in the picture' about REBT by presenting a brief account of it. For example:

'This approach to therapy is called rational emotive behaviour therapy – REBT for short. In REBT, we pay particular attention to the role of rigid beliefs (tapping forehead) in our emotional problems such as anxiety or depression. These beliefs often come in the form of absolute statements beginning "I must ..." or "I should ...". REBT holds that our emotional problems are largely self-created and therefore we have emotional responsibility for them. By working together, we can identify, challenge and change those rigid beliefs driving your problems. REBT expects you to accept responsibility for tackling your problems including the hard work and discomfort in overcoming them. REBT's focus is on how your problems are being maintained in the present rather than how they developed in the past.'

Your clients are not expected to understand or agree with this account of REBT when first presented with it. However, it does orientate them to the major themes in REBT: the thought–feeling link, collaboration, emotional and therapeutic responsibility, here-and-now focus. Of course, some clients might protest that others cause their emotional problems or 'How can you possibly understand my present problems without going back to the past?' To avoid prolonged discussion and thereby delay problem assessment, it is probably best to suggest to clients that these and other objections can be answered by showing REBT in action.

Telling their stories

Obviously clients come to therapy with a story to tell about their problems but you do not need an exhaustive amount of information or have to listen patiently until they 'run out of steam' before you start constructing an ABC analysis of their presenting problems. Wessler and Wessler (1980, p. 69) observe that 'before they [clients] will work on problems or their own belief systems, they want to complain, whine, emote, and generally say what concerns them. We find it more effective to let them do so than force them into rigid uses of the ABC model. However, we would not ordinarily devote more than a half a session to such expression of feelings.'

If you believe that your client is presenting too much information, or the information given is unnecessary to understand the problem (e.g. what the client was watching on television last night) or the client is rambling and long-winded, then as part of REBT's active-directive 'get on with it' approach you will need to intervene to start modelling specificity for the client. Specificity requires clear and precise information in understanding your client's problems:

Michael: What problem would you like to talk about?

John: Well, I suppose it's ... well, my mate said I should get some help. I was talking to him about this the other night in the pub and his girlfriend was there too – she's a very nice and understanding woman but she's got her own problems as well. Anyway, where was I? Oh yeah, I was talking to my mate who I've known for a long time and, as I said, he said I should get some help for it. You always think that talking to your mates will help you sort things out but it doesn't always, does it? I think they are too close to you, aren't they? My brother's mate is always bending his ear about something or other. My brother also thinks I should get some help for it.

Michael: May I stop you there?

John: Okay.

Michael: What's the 'it' both your friend and brother say you need help with?

John: I was just talking to them about it.

Michael: It's good to have friends and a brother to confide in. Now in REBT we like to encourage clients to provide specific information relating to the actual problem so we can be clear about what we're dealing with. So could you sum up in a sentence or two the actual problem you want help with – the 'it' in other words?

By asking for permission to interrupt, the therapist prevents the client from rambling on, emphasizes the need for information about the actual problem and starts training the client in the procedures of REBT; in this instance, an early problem-solving focus. If the client's long-windedness goes unchecked in the early stages of therapy, such behaviour may be much more difficult to rein in later on and militate against teaching successfully REBT's psychoeducational model of emotional problem-solving. In REBT, clients follow the therapist, not the other way round, if they are to understand and implement the ABCDE model.

Clients might present their problems in a number of other ways. For example:

1. in a neat package, e.g. 'I'm depressed since I lost my job.' This statement acts as an invitation to explore the depression further by asking 'What are you depressed about since losing your job?'
2. in a vague way, e.g. 'It's something about being the centre of attention, I think.' Turning vagueness into clarity can begin with the question, 'What goes through your mind when you are the centre of attention?' If the client replies 'nothing', you can try another tack by attempting to elicit how they feel or behave in such a situation. Using imagery to recreate the situation in your client's mind can be an effective technique for uncovering 'hot' (emotionally charged) cognitions and producing strong affect (emotion).
3. with uncertainty, e.g. 'I'm not sure what the problem is or even if I should be here at all.' In order to develop a problem focus, you can ask your client if there are areas in her life where she does not function as well as she would like to or if she is currently unhappy about something. The client might believe that only 'very serious problems' deserve therapeutic help which could explain her doubts about sitting in your office. If this is the case, explain that tackling 'small' problems now can prevent them from growing into bigger ones later.
4. burdened down, e.g. 'I seem to have so many worries I don't know where to start. I feel overwhelmed.' With this client, you can write down his worries so they form a problem list which can be 'ticked off' as the client learns to manage them in the course of therapy. The client

can be asked which problem he would like to start with, but if he seems unsure, you can suggest one. Picking a problem to start teaching the ABC model is more important than prolonged indecisiveness in attempting to select the most serious one.

Developing a cognitive conceptualization of the client's problem (CCCP)

This means that the clinical focus in the assessment stage of therapy is aimed at uncovering the most relevant irrational beliefs maintaining clients' emotional problems (e.g. a client's depression-inducing belief is revealed as 'Because my wife left me, which she absolutely shouldn't have done, this means I'm nothing without her.') . This process begins with asking for a problem and obtaining a clear understanding of it:

John: Well, if I was to try and put it into a sentence or two, it's about not getting on with things.

Michael: What specific things are you not getting on with?

John: Well, things like losing weight, going down the gym, looking for a more interesting job. Things like that.

Michael: What prevents you from doing these things?

John: I'm not sure why but I get angry with myself for not getting on with things. That's why I've come to see you so you can give me a kick up the backside to get things moving in my life.

Michael: Well, if we can discover what holds you back, you can deliver the kick yourself. Now we need a specific example to analyse in order to gain an initial understanding of your procrastination otherwise we will just go round in circles talking about your problems in general terms. You've mentioned three things, so which one shall we use first?

John: Losing weight.

In the above extract, the client has discussed his problem ('not getting on with things') in broad terms. You need to move from a general description of the problem to the specific contexts in which it occurs in order to collect precise information about its ABC elements. Also, at this point I (MN) avoided discussing his anger regarding his procrastination because this is highly likely to be a consequence of his procrastination and not the cause of it. The cognitive and emotive factors underlying his procrastination need to be revealed:

Michael: Okay, now imagine you are going to start your weight reduction programme this afternoon and you are committed to keeping to it. You are not going to put it off any longer. Now how are you feeling?

John: Well, sitting here now and thinking about it, I feel good. I look forward to starting it.

Michael: So why are you depriving yourself of feeling good by putting off losing weight?

John: I don't know. It seems a strange thing to do.

Michael: Well, let's change the location from the safety of my office to sitting at home all alone – you live alone, don't you?

John: Yes, that's right.

Michael: Now close your eyes and imagine sitting at home all alone. You're going to start your weight reduction programme in the next hour. Are you still feeling good?

John: No. That's gone. I'm feeling cold and shaky. Very uneasy.

Michael: Do you know which emotion you're experiencing?

John: I'm not sure. I just feel on edge now.

Establishing the presence of an unhealthy negative emotion

It is important that you elicit an unhealthy negative emotion for examination, not just any emotion the client nominates (see Table 1.1). Some clients might say they feel, for example, disappointed or annoyed by certain frustrations or setbacks they have suffered. If these emotions are underpinned by flexible and non-extreme beliefs, then these would be viewed as adaptive in the circumstances. Then the question would need to be asked: why does the client want to change these feelings? On the other hand, it is highly likely that clients' feeling language will be different from REBT's emotional vocabulary and that disappointed and annoyed are actually hurt and anger respectively or refer to other unhealthy negative emotions. Therefore it is very important to agree on and adhere to a shared feeling language throughout the course of therapy.

Also, clients often report their feelings in vague terms such as 'bad', 'stressed out' or 'upset'. What emotions do these terms refer to? As specificity is a guiding principle in REBT, you will need to pinpoint the unhealthy negative emotion(s) contained within these terms. If the client is unable to help, you can obtain a behavioural description which might indicate which emotion is implicated. For example, avoidance in anxiety, withdrawal in depression and sulking in hurt. A more sophisticated means of achieving this goal is to listen for the inferential themes embedded in clients' accounts of their problems. An example of these themes appears in Table 2.1.

Table 2.1: Inferential themes

Emotion	Inferential theme
Anger	Transgressed against, e.g. a person's wishes for peace and quiet are frequently thwarted by her neighbour's loud music
Anxiety	Threat or danger, e.g. a student is reluctant to speak in class in case he gives the wrong answer and is perceived by others as being a fool
Depression	Loss of value, e.g. when her husband leaves her for a younger woman, the wife considers that the loss of the relationship is a great one
Envy	Others experience the good fortune which the person lacks and therefore covets, e.g. a man sneers at his friend's success in attracting women and declares 'I could go out with as many women as he does if I wanted to'
Guilt	Moral violation, e.g. a religious man who commits adultery considers that he has disregarded a central biblical injunction
Hurt	Wronged, e.g. a woman who is passed over for promotion perceives that she has been betrayed by her company for not rewarding her long-standing hard work and loyalty
Jealousy	Threat to present relationship posed by another person, e.g. a man becomes increasingly suspicious when he interprets his wife's behaviour towards his brother as flirtatious
Shame	Public disclosure of weakness, e.g. a man who panics in a crowded lift when it stops between floors sees himself exposed as a weakling in the minds of others

Armed with these inferential themes in emotional disorders, you are more likely to have a greater success in pinpointing the unhealthy negative emotion if the client is unable to help you. For example, a client who says she feels upset over her husband's thoughtlessness in forgetting to buy her a birthday present when she always remember his birthdays is probably feeling hurt because she believes she has been treated unfairly by him. Also, confusion between feeling states (e.g. 'I'm not sure if it's guilt or shame to be honest. What's the difference?') can be cleared up by explaining the themes to your clients.

Distinguishing between thoughts and feelings

As REBT is primarily a cognitively-orientated theory of emotions, it is vital that you teach your clients the differences between thoughts and feelings as it is the former that changes the latter. For example, when a woman says 'I feel that my friends are against me', just because she uses the word 'feel' it does not, in REBT terms, turn the sentence into a statement of her feelings. To elicit an emotion regarding this situation, you will need to ask, for example: 'How do you feel when you believe that your friends are against you?' Often clients will reply with another thought, e.g. 'I feel that I haven't done anything wrong to justify such behaviour towards me.' Ask again how she feels about this and, this time, she might reply 'angry and hurt'.

If some clients persist in providing thoughts when you are asking for feelings, you will need to be explicit in what you are asking for, e.g. 'What I'm seeking from you is an emotion such as depression, anger or guilt. Emotions can usually be expressed in one word.' When clients do express their feelings, as opposed to their thoughts, these 'are not open to dispute; they are phenomenological experiences for which only the individual has data. You cannot argue with such subjective states, whereas thoughts, beliefs and opinions are open to challenge' (Walen, DiGiuseppe and Dryden, 1992, p. 98).

As noted in Chapter 1, C in the ABC model refers to both emotional and behavioural consequences. As REBT is primarily concerned with emotional problem-solving (e.g. encouraging a client to move from depression to sadness by re-evaluating her depressogenic thinking), exploration of behavioural Cs is of secondary importance. These Cs can often be viewed as safety behaviours to protect clients from experiencing unpleasant feelings or sensations (procrastination can be seen as a safety behaviour).

When you are seeking to locate an emotional C or discussing one that has already been revealed, avoid asking questions which reinforce A–C thinking, i.e. that events or other people directly cause our emotional reactions, e.g. 'How does your colleague's behaviour make you feel?' or 'So your colleague's behaviour makes you feel angry?' A–C thinking under-mines the principle and practice of emotional responsibility. As early as you can in therapy, teach your clients B–C thinking, i.e. that our emotional problems are largely self-induced, e.g. 'How do you feel when your colleague behaves in that way?' or 'How do you make yourself angry when your colleague behaves like that?'

Both you and your clients' use of language will need to be monitored throughout therapy to ensure that B–C thinking is emphasized while A–C thinking is phased out. Do expect some sort of struggle from your clients over this issue as you are presenting them with a paradigmatic shift in their understanding of emotional causation, e.g. 'You mean to tell me that all these years I've been angry about my boss's behaviour and my anger is mostly down to me, not him. You must be joking!'

At the end of the last section of dialogue, John described his feelings in terms of physical sensations ('cold, shaky, on edge'). The task now is to identify the emotional state that these physical sensations are connected with:

Michael: When you say you're feeling 'on edge', this can refer to being irritable, restless or tense. Does one of these strike more of a chord with you?

John: I'm definitely tense.

Michael: Okay. Now people can be tense because they are excited about something that is going to happen to them or they are worried or nervous about something unpleasant or bad happening to them. Which one is it for you?

John: Oh, definitely nervous.

Michael: So can we include your physical sensations and nervousness under the banner of anxiety?

John: Yes you can. I am anxious about losing weight. So that's the problem, is it?

Michael: Well, we've established that if you did start a weight reduction programme you would feel anxious. Why you would be anxious about it we haven't yet discovered, and this is the next step.

Assessing the activating event

This task is to discover what the client is most disturbed about in relation to the activating event (A). A key technique used for discovering this is called inference chaining. Inference chaining links the client's personally significant inferences about the A in order to find the one (sometimes called the critical A) which triggers the client's irrational belief (B) which then, in turn, directly leads to her emotional reaction at C (for further methods of finding the critical A, see Neenan and Dryden, 1999).

This technique combines speed and depth in rapidly taking clients from the periphery to the centre of their emotional disturbances by asking a series of carefully crafted 'Let's assume ... then what?' questions. It is important that you temporarily assume that each inference in the chain is true in order to understand the client's logic. Therefore do not dispute at this stage or provide reassurance if the client becomes upset as this will halt the chain and you will lose the 'scent' of the critical A. Also look for verbal, affective and behavioural clues (e.g. respectively, voice dropping, emotional intensity, increasing agitation) that signal you are on the right track of the critical A (clients can also send the same signals but for different reasons, e.g. not being listened to). Finally, use verbal economy in asking these questions; verbosity and other verbal clutter can quickly obscure the most relevant pathways to take in search of the critical A. Verbal economy can be described as the use of a few pointed words or phrases by the therapist to elicit emotionally charged and clinically relevant inferences from the client. None of the aforementioned points is followed in this extract:

Therapist: So you get angry when your girlfriend turns up late. Why are you so angry?

[Instead of questioning the client's emotion, the therapist should ask for example 'What are you angry about when she turns up late?']

Client: She's getting at me.

Therapist: Maybe there are things going on with her that you need to ask her about. That's why she seems to be getting at you. We often communicate our dissatisfactions in indirect ways. So she could be telling you that she is not receiving enough attention from you. That could be a more plausible explanation, could it not?

[Instead of providing reassurance through unasked-for hypotheses, the next question is 'And if she is... ?']

Client: (raising his voice) No! I know her much better than you do. She's telling me that she's gone off me.

Therapist: Now what evidence can you produce to support that statement? When we're emotionally upset this distorts the way we see things including our relationships.

[Again, the therapist has only to ask: 'And if she has...?' instead of disputing the client's inference. The therapist pays no attention to the client's verbal clues that he is displeased with her behaviour. This inference chain is going nowhere.]

Bearing the above points in mind, let us return to John and see how his inference chain unravels:

Michael: What is anxiety-provoking in your mind about starting the weight reduction programme?

[The question emphasizes emotional responsibility and invites the first inference from the client.]

John: Well, I suppose that I'm going to lose weight. Sounds strange, doesn't it?

Michael: If you do lose weight, then what?

[I avoid getting drawn into a discussion regarding John's 'strange' response as this could lead to a loss of focus for both of us.]

John: I'll feel happier and fitter.

Michael: And if you do ...?

John: I'll feel that I should be doing more with my life.

Michael: Such as ...?

John: Well, the most obvious example would be to find a woman.

Michael: And if you do find a woman ...?

John: Obviously I hope it works out well.

Michael: If it does work out well, would you still be anxious?

[Here the inference chain needs to be manipulated to decide if the anxiety is associated with a future relationship that does or does not 'work out well'. If the anxiety is associated with both outcomes, then both need to be examined to establish which one is more keenly felt and therefore dealt with first.]

John: No, I would be happy.

Michael: Okay, let's assume that it doesn't work out well ... what would that actually involve?

[I am seeking clarification to refine the A as much as possible.]

John: (voice drops, eyes moisten) Well, that she doesn't want me after initially going out with me. She's dumped me.

[The change in John's demeanour indicates I am probably close to the critical A.]

Michael: And if she has dumped you ...?

John: Then why did I bother in the first place?

Michael: What do you mean by 'why did I bother in the first place?'?

[I am seeking to turn John's self-addressed question into an unambiguous statement.]

John: Losing the weight was a complete waste of time.

Michael: Because ...?

John: Because it proves what I already know about myself.

Michael: Which is ...?

John: That I'm unlovable ... (his voice trails off).

Michael: (quietly) So would you say that what you are most anxious about with regard to losing weight is future rejection which will confirm in your mind that you are unlovable? Have I understood you?

John: Yes, that's it exactly. (defensively) Wouldn't everyone be anxious about rejection?

[John confirms that I have simultaneously revealed the critical A and a derivative belief based on self-depreciation. I don't respond to John's question at the present time because of his mood change but note it for possible later use as an example to teach emotional responsibility.]

Michael: How are you feeling at the moment?

John: (tries to smile) Depressed. That's why I'm reluctant to lose weight and do those other things as they will all end in disaster.

[As depression is evident, I probe for any suicidal ideas that may have been activated. John says that he has such ideas 'very occasionally' but it is not an issue he wants to discuss at the present time.]

Michael: To return to your procrastination: this protects you from experiencing that disaster you mentioned.

John: Well, it does, but I don't feel much happier living on my own. It's no real protection.

Michael: I agree it's no real protection. You now need to decide what you want to do about what we've uncovered.

Goal-setting

In the initial assessment, there are usually two goal-setting stages:

1. when the client states his problem and goal in general terms; and
2. after the A has been explored through, for example, inference chaining and the problem and goal have been made specific.

The above extract demonstrates what often happens when exploring anxiety: by encouraging clients to imagine unpleasant future events actually occurring, this brings these events into their immediate present and often results in a different emotion coming to the fore: in John's case, anxiety is replaced by depression. This emotional shift is accompanied by a change in the thematic content of the inference chain: the feared future threat contained in anxiety becomes an imagined reality and thereby turns in to the self-devaluation of depression. As two emotional Cs have been uncovered, anxiety and depression, the next step is to ask John which emotion he would like to work on first.

Short-term v. long-term goals

Clients may opt for short-term goals because they involve less work and discomfort and bring immediate results. Such short-termism often perpetuates clients' problems rather than removes them, e.g. a drug addict moves from one town to another in order to get away from the 'drug scene' but quickly relapses in her new location. REBT encourages clients to pursue goals that are more likely to endure through philosophical restructuring (removing rigid musts and absolute shoulds and their extreme derivatives) rather than 'quick fixes', e.g. challenging and changing the client's belief that she needs drugs to solve her problems, helping her to develop more constructive problem-solving methods and exploring the advantages and disadvantages of moving to a new area.

Serenity in the face of adversity

This goal usually involves clients saying they want to feel, for example, 'calm', 'relaxed', or 'indifferent' about unpleasant life events. Such a goal often involves self-denial: why suppress one's understandable wishes for bad events not to occur? A possible reason may be that clients are unable to think rationally about such events and therefore become emotionally disturbed about them; hence their desire to feel calm or indifferent. You can suggest to your clients that there is a middle way between disturbance and denial: to accept the reality of events and distinguish between what can be changed and what cannot.

'More' or 'less' goals

This refers to client statements such as 'I want to be more assertive with my friends' or 'I want to feel less guilty when I say "no" to my children.' With the first statement, what prevents him from being more assertive? He might be anxious, for example, about speaking up in case he incurs his friends' disapproval. The goal would be to remove the anxiety in order to allow his assertiveness to emerge. With the second statement, in REBT terms, feeling less guilty still implies holding on to an irrational belief even if the must is expressed in a milder form. Remorse would be the preferred REBT alternative.

However, if the client insists that 'feeling less guilty' is the way she wants to feel – 'I don't know how remorse would feel' – then you can use her term to explain how a flexible and non-extreme belief system can be developed from it, e.g. 'Feeling less guilty could now mean not calling yourself a bad mother because saying "no" is very important for children to hear in order for them to learn how to cope constructively with disappointment and frustration in their life. Does that make any sense to you?'

Unrealistic goals

Some clients might say 'I never want to experience another panic attack' or 'I want to ensure that everyone has a favourable opinion of me.' These statements probably contain implicit irrationalities which can be teased out by asking, for example, 'What if you do experience another panic attack at a later date?' (possible reply: 'I couldn't bear it if I had another one'); and 'What if some people don't view you favourably?' (possible reply: 'This will prove there is something wrong with me which I can never overcome'). The first client's goals need to be expressed along the dimensions of frequency, intensity and duration, e.g. infrequent panic attacks instead of daily ones. The second client's goals should focus on developing greater self-acceptance rather than seeking universal approval. If you do go along with such unrealistic goals, you are suggesting that you can deliver whatever the client wants!

Process at the expense of outcome

Some clients come to therapy to immerse themselves in self-exploration rather than setting specific goals for change. For example, a client I (MN) once saw wanted to investigate 'every thought that passes through my mind in order to understand its significance – e.g., "why did I think that now rather than later?"' For this kind of client, REBT is probably contraindicated. However, some clients can be shifted from process to outcome by suggesting, for example, 'You say you want to understand why you're in this mess, but what goals would you need to get out of it? Working towards such goals not only pulls you out of the mess but also helps to understand how you got into it.'

Guidelines for goal-setting

A useful acronym to guide goal selection is SMART:

Specific	e.g. 'I want to be unafraid in the presence of spiders'.
Measurable	pencil and paper tests, experiments, client self-reports, are some ways to measure if progress is being made.
Achievable	is there a reasonable expectation that the goal can be attained? Obviously you will need to teach skills to your clients if their goals are to be realized.
Realistic	this needs to be based on the client's history and personality, e.g. a man who describes himself as a 'born worrier' is being unrealistic when he describes his goal 'to be completely free from worry'.
Time-bound	can clients' goals be reached within the time they are prepared to spend in therapy? If clients want to maintain their treatment gains, then the time required outside of therapy will be lifelong.

To return to John, I now need to discuss his goals for change:

Michael: We have two emotions to tackle: anxiety and depression. Which emotion would you like to tackle first?

John: I don't know. If you could wave a magic wand and make sure that I'm not rejected by any woman I go out with, then I wouldn't feel anxious or depressed.

Michael: That's obviously unachievable and unrealistic. You're putting the responsibility for sorting out your problems into the hands of others instead of taking responsibility for them yourself.

John: What can I do then? Wait an eternity to ensure that the woman I go out with won't reject me?

Michael: How will you feel while you're waiting an eternity for the right woman?

John: Miserable, and not to mention all the time I'll waste.

Michael: You're wasting time now through your procrastination. Look, you could make a commitment to learn self-acceptance and thereby stop condemning yourself as 'unlovable'. Learning self-acceptance would mean getting rid of self-labelling.

John: How do I do that? It won't be easy – I've been doing it for a long time.

Michael: I agree it probably won't be easy but learning self-acceptance, warts and all, is more likely to help you tackle your emotional problems successfully.

John: How is that going to help me? It won't stop me being rejected.

Michael: You are right that it won't stop rejection but it can certainly stop the self-condemnation and depression that follow and, instead, lead to self-acceptance and healthy feelings of sadness about being rejected as I'll show you in a moment.

John: Hmm. I see what you're getting at.

Michael: What am I getting at?

John: Well, I presumably won't be afraid of being rejected ...

Michael: ... but if you are rejected ...?

John: I don't have to condemn myself and feel depressed.

Michae: What healthy feelings would you like to experience instead?

John: Hmm. I'm not sure.

Michael: In REBT, we suggest sadness as the emotional alternative to depression because you accept the grim reality, in your case rejection, without putting yourself down while continuing to seek other partners.

John: Well, I suppose I could try it on like a new suit to see if it feels right.

Michael: If you don't like the term sadness obviously use your own. Try to ensure that it reflects acceptance of the situation as well as of yourself.

John: How will I know if I'm becoming more self-accepting?

Michael: By developing a belief system based on it and putting this into daily practice by doing things you usually avoid.

John: Like what?

Michael: We can discuss that when we come to setting the first homework task. For now, is self-acceptance a goal you wish to pursue?

John: Yes. I'll give it a chance.

Michael: Good. You can crack this problem if you work at it. Now I'd like to turn to some other issues if I may.

John: Okay.

As the above extract illustrates, goal-setting can involve a prolonged discussion which includes gaining a commitment from clients to accept responsibility for change, weighing up the advantages and disadvantages of goals selected and providing encouragement that progress can be made.

Meta-emotional problems

One of the unique features of REBT is its emphasis on meta-emotional disturbances or what some REBT therapists refer to as secondary emotional disturbances (Ellis and Bernard, 1985); in other words, to disturb ourselves about our primary emotional disturbances, e.g. angry about feeling jealous; ashamed about feeling anxious. It is important that you look for the possible presence of these meta-emotional problems as they can impede or prevent progress being made in therapy. The use of questions combined with illustrations can help to uncover meta-emotional problems: 'Are there any other issues or feelings that might prevent or distract you from discussing your panic attacks at work? What I mean by this is that some clients feel angry or ashamed about having a problem in the first place as well as discussing it with a stranger such as myself. Does that ring any bells with you?' If a meta-emotional problem is detected, then the following three criteria can be employed to determine if you should focus on it first (Dryden and DiGiuseppe, 1990):

1. If the meta-emotional problem interferes significantly with the work you are trying to do on the original one, e.g. the client frequently erupts into anger over the hurt he feels at being passed over for promotion. Such interference can occur both in and out of the counselling session.
2. If, clinically speaking, the meta-emotional problem is the more important of the two: the meta-emotional problem now becomes the primary focus of clinical attention.
3. If your client can see the sense of working on his meta-emotional problem first.

Some clients may appear reluctant to discuss their problems, downplay the apparent importance of them, discuss them in purely intellectual terms or seem to be 'wasting time' in therapy. The emotion at work here could be shame, e.g. the client fears being seen as pathetic by the therapist if he admits to crying. If you suspect the presence of shame, suggest to your client that counselling is a safe place to test his belief that he will experience humiliation when he discloses his problem. Shame or other meta-emotional problems can emerge at any time in therapy, so be on the alert for them.

At this point in the assessment process, I probe for any meta-emotional problems John might be experiencing:

Michael: We've agreed to look at the depression you feel about rejection and putting yourself down, now do you experience any other feelings associated with being depressed, like anger or shame, for example?

John: I feel ashamed.

Michael: Okay. Now will the shame prevent or distract you in some way from focusing upon me teaching you REBT and helping you to tackle your depression?

John: I don't think so but how can I really know?

Michael: If you spend more time preoccupied with your shame than you do listening to me!

John: Okay, sounds sensible. I'll let you know if I stop paying attention.

Michael: Good.

Teaching the B–C connection

This step is crucial if your client is to understand and carry out REBT: namely, that emotional disturbance is largely determined by our irrational beliefs and not externally created. The concept of emotional responsibility mentioned earlier in therapy now takes centre stage. If you have a whiteboard in your office, you may want to write the ABC model on it. In teaching the B–C connection, it is preferable to keep your story simple, clear and vivid as this is more likely to help your clients to grasp the significance of your story. In our experience, those REBTers who opt for complicated stories are apt to confuse their clients as well as themselves, so keep in mind that B–C can also stand for Brief–Clear connection in teaching emotional responsibility.

You can pick a story unrelated to your client's presenting problem (e.g. guilt about having an affair) as she may not be able to employ sufficient detachment while listening to your story if it is similar to her own. If the client displays too much detachment then the story could be uninteresting and/or uninvolving; if this is the case, then use some aspect of the client's experience as a teaching example. Alternatively, you can use your client's material if it will make more of an impact, e.g. a client states that everyone would feel just as angry as he does if they had to work with his boss – this can provide the 'way in' to teach him about idiosyncratic emotional reactions to the same event. If using personal material reinforces the client's A–C thinking and/or is too emotionally arousing (e.g. 'Of course they would all be bloody angry!'), then switch to a story that the client can view in a less excited manner.

Having established that John is not currently preoccupied with any meta-emotional problems, I am now ready to teach him the B–C connection by using something he said earlier in therapy:

Michael Do you remember saying when we were analysing your anxiety that everyone would be anxious about being rejected?

John: Yes, I do. Well, they would, wouldn't they?

Michael: Well, let's explore it a little. I want to show you how it is our beliefs about events, not the events themselves, that largely determine our emotional reactions to these events. I'm going write all this on the whiteboard for greater clarity. Now imagine two men who fancy the same woman and are going to ask her out. Now the possibility of rejection is exactly the same for both of them and we can call this the activating event or A. Do you agree?

John: Yes. So far, so good.

Michael: Now at B or beliefs about the A, the first man believes (with heavy emphasis) 'She *must* not reject me because if she does, this will prove that I'm worthless.'

John: I can understand that!

Michael: Now the second man believes (with equal emphasis) 'I don't *want* her to reject me but there is no reason unfortunately why she must not. If she does, I'm certainly not going to put myself down because of it. Instead, I'm going to accept myself.' Now which of the two is more likely to feel anxious at C and why?

John: Obviously the first.

Michael: Because ...?

John: Because he's insisting that she mustn't reject him and he is worthless if she does. I'm definitely man number one.

Michael: How will man number two feel, do you think?

John: He'll be concerned because he won't want to be rejected but he won't be *too* bothered about it.

Michael: Why?

John: Well, because it isn't all or nothing with him like it is with the first man. He accepts that he might be rejected.

Michael: That's right. The first man holds a *must*, a rigid belief (B) about A which leads to anxiety at C. The second man expresses a *want*, a flexible belief (B) about A which leads to feeling healthy concern at C rather than anxiety. When you convert a want into a must you're usually heading for emotional trouble. Does that appear to make sense?

John: (nodding) Seems quite plausible. Is that what I'm doing?

Michael: We'll discover if you are in a moment.

Uncovering the client's irrational belief and linking this to his emotional disturbance

In Chapter 1, we noted how an irrational belief is composed of two parts: the premise and derivative. To recap, the premise is an unconditional must or absolute should statement often expressed as a demand or command we make on ourselves, others or world/life conditions; the derivative is the conclusion of that statement. REBT identifies three major derivatives: awfulizing, low frustration tolerance (LFT) and depreciation of self, others or world/life conditions. For example, 'I must always have things easy in my life (premise) because if they're not, my life will be horrible' (derivative based on awfulizing).

The meanings of should

REBT hypothesizes that rigid musts, shoulds, oughts, have to's and got to's are usually to be found at the core of emotional disturbance. As we have stressed previously, it is important not to assume that these words are automatically disturbance-producing. It is important for you to listen carefully to the meaning of the word if you want to understand its intent, the context in which it is used and the emotional state of the client in order to determine if the word has pathological properties.

The word 'should' is particularly troublesome in trying to ascertain its meaning as it can be used in a number of ways which include:

1. as a preference, e.g. 'You should (preferably) look carefully when you cross the road in order to reduce your chances of having an accident';
2. as a recommendation, e.g. '(I recommend that) you should read that book; it's really gripping';
3. as a probability, e.g. 'You should (in all probability) get paid on the last Wednesday of every month';
4. as an absolute, e.g. 'You *absolutely* should never trust anyone.'

REBT argues that it is only absolute shoulds that are correlated with emotional disturbance.

In order to avoid or reduce the confusion arising from the multiple meanings of the word 'should', we suggest you substitute 'must' for 'should' as this better conveys rigidity of thought, e.g. 'When you say "she should pay more attention to me", do you mean it in the sense of "she must pay more attention to me"?' Unless you learn to make these discrim-inations, 'time may be lost in stamping out irrelevant shoulds (i.e. shoulds that are not at the core of the client's emotional disturbance), and the therapist may merely succeed in developing a new unexamined taboo ("I should not say 'should'")' (Walen, DiGiuseppe and Dryden, 1992, p. 116).

Questions to assess irrational beliefs

In uncovering the client's irrational or self-defeating belief, you can use open-ended or theory-driven questions. Open-ended questions encourage your clients to think for themselves about their patterns of thinking and the connections with their emotional problems. Open-ended questions also allow you to determine how much of the REBT material clients have retained and how accurate this retention is. An example of an open-ended question would be: 'Given your partner's ingratitude at A, what are you saying to yourself at B to feel angry at C?' In our experience, the question above will usually be answered with an inference (assump-tion) rather than an irrational belief (demand), e.g. 'I think he's gone off me' v. 'He mustn't treat me like this!' If this is the case, it is important to teach your client that inferences in REBT are peripheral to emotional disturbance while irrational beliefs are central to it. Feedback can be sought by asking the same question again to see if there is a different answer – this time based on demands.

If the answer is the same or similar, then you will probably need to ask a theory-driven question. This one is taken from REBT theory and directs the client to the answer required, e.g. 'What *demand* are you making about your partner's ingratitude at A that leads you to feel angry at C?' Again in our experience, despite giving the client the answer on a plate, some clients will answer with a preference, e.g. 'I wish he wouldn't behave like that.' As with the distinction between inferences and beliefs, further teaching is required to emphasize the differences in outlook between preferences and demands. Theory-driven questions seem to substantiate one of the criticisms levelled against REBT that it tells clients what to think.

However, while REBTers teach their clients the ABCDE model as a means of emotional problem-solving, they cannot impose the model on them for the simple reason that clients make the final choice about the credibility and applicability of the model. Ethical REBT therapists make the REBT model of emotional disturbance and therapy explicit to their clients and elicit their informed consent to proceed before fully involving them in the therapeutic process (Dryden, 1999a).

I now return to John to assess his irrational belief and connect it to his unhealthy negative emotion of depression. I need to draw his attention back to the critical A we uncovered during the inference chaining process (if you remember, his derivative irrational belief based on self-depreciation was also uncovered):

Michael: Let me recap. It is our beliefs (tapping forehead) about events, not the events themselves, that determine our emotional reactions. Okay?

John: I'm following.

Michael: Demands in the form of rigid musts and absolute shoulds can lead to emotional disturbance while preferences and wishes can lead to emotional problems but fall short of disturbance. Now when we were using inference chaining to explore your anxiety, do you remember what you were most anxious about?

John: Being rejected.

Michael: And calling yourself what?

John: Unlovable.

Michael: Okay. Now we've agreed to tackle your depression first: either you imagine you have been rejected or it has actually occurred. What are you telling yourself about the rejection that leads you to being depressed?

John:I wish I had not been rejected.

[He replies with a flexible (rational) belief which would not, in REBT terms, lead to him feeling depressed.]

Michael: If you remember the example of the two men facing possible rejection, what was the key difference in their beliefs about being rejected?

John: Well, the one who was anxious was being rigid because he was saying 'She mustn't reject me' and the other one wasn't too bothered about it because he wasn't insisting on it.

Michael: A rigid must versus a flexible want. Now if you believed 'I wish I had not been rejected', how would you feel?

John: Down but not depressed if you see what I mean.

Michael: Okay. Now we know that you get depressed, not down, when you've been rejected, so is it really a want you are expressing?

John: No, I suppose not. I'm really saying, 'She shouldn't have rejected me.'

Michael: Can we be clear about that 'should': is it expressed as a regret about her decision or a demand that she absolutely shouldn't have done what she did?

John: She absolutely shouldn't have rejected me.

Michael: But as she did, what does that mean about you?

John: I'm unlovable. That part was always clear to me.

Michael: So I'll write on the board your self-defeating belief: 'I absolutely shouldn't have been rejected but as I was, this proves I'm unlovable.'

John: I can remember the last time I was rejected, I wasn't expressing any regret. I was howling to myself 'She shouldn't have done it!' That belief does make sense (pointing at the board). We've come a long way from discussing losing weight.

Michael: We sure have (both gaze in silence at the whiteboard for several seconds).

I now need to elicit from John an explicit connection between his irrational belief at B and his depression at C; if he makes this connection, then my next step is to probe as to how emotional change can be achieved. If these connections are not made, your clients will be unsure or baffled when you start disputing their beliefs.

Michael: Now John, can you see that as long as you continue to demand that you absolutely shouldn't have been rejected but as you have been, which proves you are unlovable, you will continue to make yourself depressed?

John: I do see that.

Michael: Can you put it in your own words then?

John: Well, as long as I believe that rejection absolutely shouldn't happen to me, I'm going to be depressed when it does.

Michael: So if you want to stop feeling depressed when you're rejected and only feel down instead, what do you need to change?

John: That belief with the absolute should in it (pointing at the board).

Michael: And the idea that you are unlovable too.

From the moment I asked John for a problem to discuss, we have been working towards understanding it within the framework of a cognitive conceptualization of the client's problem (CCCP). This has now been established: namely, the irrational belief underlying his depression which is 'I absolutely shouldn't have been rejected but as I have been, this proves I am unlovable.' However, this CCCP should be seen as tentative because it is an initial conceptualization of John's problems and probably will be refined further in the light of more incoming information.

Historical perspective on present problems

REBT's primary focus is on understanding and tackling problems in the here and now rather than exploring the historical background of these problems. However, some clients will not be happy with this ahistorical emphasis and insist, for example, that 'You can't understand the present without going into the past.' Beck (1995, p. 7) suggests that

> attention shifts to the past in three circumstances: when the patient expresses a strong predilection to do so; when work directed toward current problems produces little or no cognitive, behavioral, and emotional change; or when the therapist judges that it is important to understand how and when important dysfunctional ideas originated and how these ideas affect the patient today.

This shift to the past can be part of the initial assessment of your client's problems if deemed necessary or carried out later in therapy when the client has gained some emotional stability and is less likely to become too upset when discussing historical material.

However, when conducting an historical investigation, it is important to stress to your clients that insight gained retrospectively is usually insufficient to promote therapeutic change in the present; this is accomplished by combining insight with sustained and forceful action *now* to achieve a successful problem-solving outcome.

John was staring at the whiteboard, so I asked him what he was thinking about:

John: That belief of mine (nodding towards the board) didn't just come out of the blue, did it?

Michael: True. You can trace that belief back to past events.

John: I would very much like to do that.

Michael: We can do that now or wait until you've gained some confidence in tackling your problems.

John: No, I'd really like to do that now.

Michael: Okay, but REBT advocates that we do not spend too much time in the past as actual change comes from thinking and behaving differently today.

John: I understand that and I don't want to get bogged down in the past either.

John described his parents as 'distant and not very affectionate'. He considered that there 'must be something wrong with me' and concluded that he was 'unlovable'. His slightly older brother, Peter, was apparently untroubled by his parents' behaviour and led a relatively carefree existence: 'He's been happily married for fifteen years and has three children. Why couldn't I be like him?' As he grew up, John found himself in a bind: he desperately wanted to be in a relationship to convince himself that he was lovable yet feared rejection as this would prove he was actually unlovable.

Lacking confidence in himself, he was very wary about approaching women and therefore his relationships were few and short-lived. The usual pattern was intense anxiety involved in asking someone out because he might be rejected and bouts of depression when he was. He said he lived a rather joyless existence and that was why 'I don't really bother how I look. Why bother when no one wants you?' Remaining alone afforded some protection against rejection but became a self-fulfilling prophecy that he was unwanted. However, every now and again he became 'fired up' with the idea of changing his life and making it more exciting. Hence his present self-referral for therapy.

Scott, Stradling and Dryden (1995, p. 13) suggest that 'sharing your conceptualisation of the client's difficulties gives the client a map of how he or she arrived at the present position, and also opens up the possibility that alternative routes could have been taken if the client had known then what he or she knows now'. John's childhood view of himself as unlovable can be seen as a rigid attitude towards self formed earlier in life (RASE) which then determined his outlook and behaviour. Rigid beliefs can also be constructed about others or world/life conditions. These rigid views of self, others or the world can be formed at any time in our lives and are usually triggered (but not caused) by a personally significant event(s) or trauma. In John's case, his parents' behaviour towards him:

John: That does make a lot of sense. Why couldn't I have followed my brother's route and been happy like him?

Michael: Because the rigid beliefs you constructed about yourself formed a kind of bias against yourself: you looked for evidence to support your view of being unlovable but didn't really look for evidence to discredit this idea. And that's what's been going on all these years. You can choose a different route now if you are prepared to work hard and be open-minded about testing out new behaviours.

John: I am prepared to. I'm thirty-six years old and miserable. I want to go out with some women!

Elegant v. inelegant change

As we discussed in Chapter 1, elegant change in REBT consists of giving up all rigid and extreme musts and shoulds or, at least more realistically, reducing the frequency of their operation in our lives. The elegant solution to our emotional problems is to undergo a profound philosophical change. By contrast, inelegant change is non-philosophical and considered to be superficial because it is only aimed at symptom relief (though this form of relief can be very important to some clients). With this kind of change we remain much more vulnerable to present and future episodes of emotional disturbance because our underlying disturbance-creating beliefs are left unexamined and thereby intact. REBT obviously favours the elegant solution but as Ellis (Ellis, Young and Lockwood, 1987, p. 248) points out: 'It is true that a good many therapy clients will never fully accept the elegant rational solutions of RE[B]T ... but that is hardly a reason for not trying to get them to do so! Even if only 10 or 20% of these clients will accept such solutions ... it is well worth trying to help them do this.'

I discussed with John the REBT view of elegant change:

Michael: REBT prefers individuals to strive for long-term problem-solving rather than short-term feel-good solutions. In your case, give up self-condemnation and learn self-acceptance, stop demanding you mustn't be rejected and, instead, see rejection as unfortunate but nothing more. And persist in asking women out: not one every several years but one every month until you click with someone. And stick with losing weight and getting fit so you feel and look better. Hard work and commitment to achieving these and other changes and then keeping them. Get my drift?

John: I do and it sounds good, but how do I know I will succeed with these changes?

Michael: You don't, and that's another thing you need to learn: acceptance of uncertainty. Sustained hard work is more likely, but not inevitably, to bring some rewards. I probably can guarantee one thing ...

John: I know – if I don't change I'll remain miserable.

Michael: Right.

John: Okay, I'm ready. One last thing: how long will this take?

Michael: You could be asking women out in a month or two. To maintain the changes you've made will probably require a sustained ongoing effort.

In summary, the ABCs of the initial assessment have been established; at John's request, an historical component was included in this assessment; he has opted for the elegant solution as a means of change and a rough time-scale to measure improvement has been offered. Now we need to turn our attention to discussing the process of disputing irrational beliefs.

Chapter 3
Disputing

In this chapter, we consider, among other things, the importance of multi-modal (cognitive, imaginal, behavioural and emotive) disputing in promoting belief change; typical logical, empirical and pragmatic arguments used in cognitive disputing and a demonstration of concurrent disputing whereby irrational and rational beliefs are questioned at the same time; and discriminating irrational from rational beliefs in the disputing process.

What we mean by disputing

One dictionary definition of dispute is 'quarrel'. If you did quarrel with your clients about their irrational beliefs this would quickly lead to unpleasantness and, at the very least, a rupture in the therapeutic alliance. Therefore disputing is not about being rude, offensive, abrasive, engaging in a power struggle or in-your-face confrontation, though it certainly can be robust or spirited at times.

Another dictionary definition comes close to the REBT meaning of disputing: 'question the truth or correctness or validity of (a statement, alleged fact, etc.)'. Disputing, or D in the ABCDE model, engages clients in an examination of their irrational beliefs (premise and derivative); this examination is intended to lead to the development of a rational or flexible belief system. In essence, REBT therapists want to prove to clients there is no logical and empirical support (and little pragmatic support) for their rigid and extreme beliefs, but there is such support for flexible and non-extreme beliefs. DiGiuseppe (1991, p. 173) observes that 'disputing irrational beliefs has always been at the heart of RE[B]T' and is the principal activity of experienced REBTers.

Disputing is not an open-minded process whereby the therapist could be persuaded that the client's disturbance-producing beliefs are, in fact, rational because these beliefs are highly unlikely to meet REBT's criteria for rationality (of course, your clients do not *have* to accept the REBT viewpoint and, equally, there is no reason why you *must* persuade them to think more rationally though it would be preferable for them to do so). Disputing is theory-driven in the sense that you know the client's arguments cannot hold water (e.g. 'I must have what I want in life') and therefore are invalid while rational arguments are well-founded and stand up to examination (e.g. 'There is no reason why I must have what I want in life even though it would be nice').

In a chapter called 'The Best Rational Arguments', Hauck (1980, p. 117) suggests that

> reason takes hold in most instances merely because it is so correct. However, it helps enormously to have a series of logical arguments at your fingertips which you can call upon which are so reasonable, so irrefutably right, that an opposing idea cannot exist once the rational one has been grasped.

This might be described as the acme of disputing skill and therefore a highly desirable goal that most REBTers wish to achieve.

Disputing can be seen as a form of verbal persuasion: if clients adopt the REBT view of rationality they are likely to become less disturbable and more goal-orientated. If some clients object to the term 'disputing', you can use, for example, discussing, debating, examining, questioning, re-evaluating or whatever term the client prefers, e.g. 'Let's kick around these ideas that I have.'

Belief levels

Irrational beliefs can be held at what DiGiuseppe (1991, p. 186) calls 'varying levels of abstraction'. The level of abstraction ranges from beliefs expressed in specific situations (e.g. 'He must get that report to me by noon today'), across situations (e.g. 'My friends and colleagues must not let me down') and globally (e.g. 'People must not make my life difficult'). If an irrational belief held at a general level is disputed, this will tackle a greater number of activating events the client disturbs himself about (when friends and colleagues let him down) than a belief subscribed to in a specific context (the report fails to arrive at noon). Clients can usually 'hear' and are prepared to work on their irrational beliefs in specific situations but might be reluctant to work at more abstract levels because they are not aware of holding pervasive irrational ideas. Also, it does not follow that a client who has disputed successfully a general belief will automatically dispute successfully a specific version of this general belief.

However, successful disputing of a concrete belief can encourage some clients to 'dig deeper' into their thinking to uncover a general version of the concrete belief. Ideally, you should intervene at the various levels of abstraction if far-reaching belief change is to occur.

Multimodal disputing

This means that REBT uses cognitive, behavioural, imaginal and emotive techniques in the service of belief change. As thoughts, feelings and behaviours are interdependent and interactive, change in one modality (e.g. behaviour) has effects on the other modalities. However, REBT considers cognition to be first among interdependent and interactive equals in understanding and tackling emotional distress. As Walen, DiGiuseppe and Dryden (1992, p. 16) point out: 'If distress is a product of irrational thinking, *the best way to conquer distress is to change this thinking*. Clinically, this approach is often the only (or at least the most practical) aspect of the emotional experience that we can encourage clients to change' (italics in original). Emotive, behavioural and imaginal techniques are used to support and deepen cognitive change.

REBT is selective about the techniques it uses in the disputing process as some are aimed at alleviating problems rather than removing them (e.g. distraction, relaxation, positive thinking). REBT prefers to pick techniques which encourage clients to strive for a profound philosophical and emotional change (e.g. getting into a lift thirty times in one day instead of once a week in order to overcome rapidly a lift phobia). Such techniques are designed to help clients not only feel better but also get and stay better.

REBT considers some methods to be iatrogenic (i.e. they inadvertently induce problems for clients or exacerbate their existing ones) and therefore are generally avoided: for example, showing excessive warmth to a client with strong needs for approval can lead to increasing dependence upon the therapist in the change process rather than developing independence in facing her problems.

Creative persistence is required in selecting techniques to promote belief change as it is highly unlikely you will 'hit the cognitive jackpot' with the first techniques you use. Try to discover which modality promotes optimal client learning as this is more likely to encourage clients to dispute their irrational ideas, e.g. 'I like to have a strong image in my mind then I know where I am with things' or 'I'm the kind of person who likes to be doing, not sitting about gazing at my navel.'

Cognitive disputing

Techniques used in this form of disputing are defined by Wessler and Wessler (1980, p. 113) as those 'that rely solely on verbal interchange between therapist and client (within sessions), between the client and himself (written or thinking homework), and between author and client (reading and listening to tapes as homework)'. The purpose of this verbal interchange is for your clients to think about their irrational ideas in ways that will discredit these ideas and, in turn, lead to the development of credible rational ideas. Cognitive disputing or verbal interchange relies primarily on five arguments: whether clients' beliefs are flexible or rigid, extreme or non-extreme, and questioning the logical, empirical and pragmatic status of these beliefs. Such arguments can help to turn the tide in clients' irrational thinking. The aim of therapist-led disputing is the development of self-disputing on the client's part.

Rigidity versus flexibility

With this argument, clients are invited to consider if their beliefs are rigid or flexible. Rigid beliefs usually allow no other outcome than the one demanded and therefore no room for manoeuvre if things go wrong, e.g. 'I must get that job at all costs. I will not contemplate defeat!' Such all-or-nothing thinking is likely to produce emotional disturbance when goals are not attained; in the above example, the individual experiences anger and depression when she fails to get the job and is unable to see any way of recovering 'from this devastating blow'. Even when clients see the poor results of their rigid thinking some still refuse to modify it.

I (MN) once saw a client for a period of nine months who had an anger problem over his erratic sleep pattern – 'I absolutely must have eight hours' sleep every night. I will not compromise on this issue'. I made no therapeutic headway in all the time I saw him and his sleep pattern did not improve. I would describe his adherence to his rigid beliefs as adamantine, i.e. utterly unyielding to all the arguments I employed as well as the appeals of his family, friends and GP. This example is intended to demonstrate there are degrees of rigidity you will encounter: from rigid but willing to listen to and/or explore other viewpoints to seemingly impervious to all other viewpoints.

Flexible beliefs, on the other hand, emphasize the strong desire for goal-attainment but acknowledge the possibility of setbacks and failures; if these occur, alternative plans are implemented. Such an outlook will usually produce non-disturbed negative feelings in the face of unpleasant activating events.

Extremism versus non-extremism

Extremism in REBT means a tendency to think about ourselves and events immoderately: cognitive restraint is abandoned and thinking is pushed to its outermost reaches or limits in making judgements, e.g. a man who loses his job concludes that he is utterly worthless; a woman who falls out with her daughter claims that her life is now awful. Extreme thinking is correlated with emotional disturbance.

Non-extremism is based on a moderate outlook: arguments are balanced and judgements are carefully made, e.g. a man who loses his job concludes that he is jobless but not worthless as he refrains from making his self-worth contingent upon having a job or anything else in his life; a woman who falls out with her daughter realizes that her life has become more difficult but certainly not awful. Non-extreme thinking is correlated with emotional discontent.

Logical arguments

Logic is the correct use of reasoning and has nothing to do with how we feel (Vesey and Foulkes, 1990). It is important to stress this last point as clients frequently use their feelings (though from the REBT viewpoint, it is usually thoughts that are actually referred to) as a form of reasoning, e.g. 'If I feel that I'm a failure, then it surely follows that I am one.' The basic structure of reasoning starts with a premise and reaches a conclusion from it. This form of reasoning is called deductive logic. An argument is deemed to be logical if it is impossible for the conclusion to be false if the premise is true. Obviously REBT argues, derived from its theory, that clients' irrational premises are false (e.g. 'I must never make mistakes') and there-fore the conclusions will also be false (e.g. 'but as I have made them, this means I'm incompetent') because there are no logical grounds to support unconditional musts and shoulds or global evaluations of human worth.

With regard to the above example, you could ask regarding the premise, 'How does it logically follow that because you prefer never to make mistakes therefore you must never make them?' A similar question can be asked regarding the conclusion, 'Because you have made mistakes, how then does it logically follow that you as a person are incompetent because of them?' When challenging clients' must statements, e.g. 'Why must you never make mistakes?', clients usually provide answers based on preferences, e.g. 'Because I don't want to make mistakes', 'I don't like the problems that result' or 'Of course, people prefer not to make mistakes.' You can agree with the client's preferences but point out she has not answered the question. Preferring something not to occur and then demanding that it must not occur is an illogical jump in her thinking. If clients readily concede that their thinking is not logical, you will need to ensure through feedback they do really understand the illogical nature of their irrational beliefs.

Typical questions to ask in logical disputing include:

- Does that seem like good logic to you?
- Does it logically follow that because you want it therefore you must have it?
- Can you detect any inconsistencies in your thinking?
- Are you contradicting yourself? (e.g. 'You say it's a setback in your life, so how does that lead to the end of your world?')
- You say that if your friend held that view you would regard it as unreasonable, so why is it reasonable for you to hold it?

Empirical disputing

This form of disputing asks: are your beliefs realistic? In other words, do your demands correspond with the world/life as it actually is? Clients are requested to provide evidence in support of their beliefs. REBT argues that rigid musts and shoulds do not match empirical reality. For example, if I (MN) demand that I must have blue eyes instead of brown eyes and the world is subservient to my demands, then my brown eyes would change to blue because the world would make it so. Clients often agree that such a demand is absurd, then go back to insisting that their demands are realistic, e.g. 'I must be perfect; what's wrong with that?' Again, if this client was master of the universe, then his demands would be met and obviously the thought of coming to therapy would never cross his mind. But his life provides ample evidence that he is not perfect and demanding that he must be perfect just reinforces his status as a fallible (imperfect) human being.

Sometimes in-session demonstrations can vividly illustrate empirical disputing. For example, go to the window and demand that the weather must immediately change or that the pen you are holding must not drop to the floor when you let go of it. Encourage your clients to engage in such demonstrations to reinforce reality-testing. Some clients might give examples where they demanded something and it occurred such as 'I was sitting alone at home, fed up and bored. I told the phone to ring so a friend would invite me out. And do you know what? – it rang and I was invited out!' This is evidence for a coincidence or fortuitous occurrence, not the world conforming to their demands.

When clients condemn themselves as 'worthless' or 'useless' this means, if such beliefs reflect reality, that everything they have done, are doing or will do is worthless or useless. You can point out, for example, that if they are truly useless how did they get to the session, let alone on time? How have they managed to get dressed, feed themselves etc.? Clients usually protest this is not what they mean when they call themselves 'useless', but point out to them this is exactly what is meant by their global self-depreciation. When clients report that negative events in their lives are the worst they could possibly be, suggest to them there is always something worse lurking around the corner, e.g.

Client: I might die of cancer at a young age.

Therapist: It could be worse, at least with cancer you have so many months to live, a heart attack might finish you off immediately.

As a general rule, if clients say after a few challenges that there is no evidence to support their irrational beliefs, do not be easily convinced by this answer: there is usually a lot of evidence accumulated over the years and lodged in their heads that needs to be revealed and examined by you.

Typical questions to ask in empirical disputing include:

- Where's the evidence that the world must give you what you demand?
- Prove that the world obeys your demands.
- Where is it written that life must give you what you want?
- What experiment could we devise to test if you are in fact master/mistress of the universe?
- When you say you can't stand it, how long have you actually been standing it?
- Let's assume that those bad things did happen, how would that be awful?
- If you believe you can control his/her behaviour, why then doesn't he/she respond to your demands?

Pragmatic disputing

This form of disputing focuses on the usefulness/helpfulness of subscribing to irrational beliefs, e.g. 'Where is it going to get you if you hold on to the idea that you must always succeed?' Does the belief actually help in achieving the desired goal? The point of the pragmatic dispute is to show clients all they are likely to 'hold on to' are self-defeating emotions and behaviours which interfere with or block goal-attainment. Clients are likely to provide you with a number of reasons why their ideas are useful/helpful. These can be written down on a whiteboard as advantages and then contrasted with their disadvantages. Often the disadvantages outweigh, sometimes greatly so, the advantages but the latter are viewed, for example, as protective or inspirational (e.g. 'Musts make me strive for perfection in everything I do'); hence clients' continuing attachment to them. So do not expect clients to surrender immediately their irrational beliefs just because you have identified more drawbacks than benefits.

However, having just said that, pragmatic disputing is for many clients more effective than logical or empirical disputing in initiating change because of the concreteness involved in itemizing the self-defeating consequences of retaining their irrational ideas.

Typical questions to ask in pragmatic disputing include:

- Where is it going to get you if you continue to think in this way?
- Do you think that these many drawbacks we have identified are worth the price of the few benefits associated with your belief?
- What will happen if you hang on to that must?
- Does that belief actually motivate you to reach your goal?
- You said that belief causes you so much unhappiness, so why do you cling on to it?
- Will that belief give you the results you desire?
- Is that belief really indispensable in your life?

Socratic and didactic disputing.

Dryden (1995a) states that these are the two major disputing styles. Socratic disputing involves asking questions that stimulate clients' thinking about the logical, empirical and pragmatic nature of their irrational ideas and whether these ideas are flexible or rigid, extreme or non-extreme, e.g. 'Is it realistic to demand that your friend absolutely shouldn't have slept with your wife when he has already done so?' Such questions guide clients to discover what REBTers already know: namely, there is no support or evidence for their irrational beliefs (clients, of course, can and do reject these arguments). Socratic disputing can be a painstaking process for some clients as they struggle to respond to your questions because this may be the first time in their lives they have been required to examine their beliefs.

At times, this question and answer approach will be non-productive (e.g. 'I have absolutely no idea why my belief is unrealistic'). If this is the case, you can switch to didactic disputing whereby you teach clients the REBT viewpoint on the subject under discussion. As with teaching the B–C connection, keep your lectures brief and clear – do not use these lectures to impress clients with your 'wisdom'. The point of the lecture is to establish or enhance clients' understanding of REBT and this can be gauged through feedback, e.g. 'Could you put into your own words the points I've just made? I want to be sure I've made myself clear.' Remember that clients can understand your lecture without agreeing with it; so you will need to elicit both understanding and agreement if therapy is to proceed and progress to be made.

Though both forms of disputing will be used in therapy, it is preferable to be more Socratic than didactic in order 'to let clients' brains take the strain' of concentrated thinking; too much lecturing offers some clients the chance of slipping into passivity and a succession of 'hmms' from them may indicate their attention is elsewhere.

Order in disputing

Dryden (1995a) stresses the importance of order in disputing, i.e. one belief at a time (premise or derivative) and one argument at a time, e.g. an empirical dispute aimed at a client's irrational premise 'I must be liked by everyone.' Once the client has understood, usually tentatively at this stage of disputing, that there is no empirical evidence to support her must, then switch to logical or pragmatic disputing of her premise until all three arguments have been used. Then use these arguments consecutively on her derivative belief 'If I'm not liked by everyone, then this proves I'm unlikeable.' If you continually switch between logical, empirical and pragmatic disputes and keep changing the focus from premise to derivative or vice versa, you will prevent disputing in depth on one belief target. Also, you are highly likely to confuse yourself as well as your client! Through the disputing process you will usually discover which arguments your clients find the most credible or persuasive and on which belief they have the most positive impact, e.g. pragmatic disputes targeting the derivative belief.

Challenging clients' irrational beliefs will not automatically produce rational alternatives. As DiGiuseppe (1991, p. 181) observes: 'People frequently hold on to beliefs that they know are logically flawed and do not lead to accurate predictions of reality, but no alternative ideas are available to replace the flawed idea ... People do not give up ideas, regardless of the evidence against the idea, unless they have an alternative to it.' Once an irrational belief has been isolated and the client has agreed to tackle it, ask him what alternative belief he would like to endorse. If he has difficulty in suggesting one, help him construct one, e.g. 'Would you like to face setbacks in your life without disturbing yourself about them? (client nods). So what would you need to say to yourself in order to achieve this?'

Remember that a rational belief is not immediately accepted and acted upon just as a long-standing irrational belief is not abruptly discarded and acted against. The process of belief change is usually more gradual as clients weaken their adherence to irrational ideas by persistently thinking, acting, and feeling against them and strengthen their commitment to rational ideas by persistently thinking, acting and feeling in support of them.

Some difficulties in disputing

Disputing can be a daunting prospect, particularly for novice REBTers. Any number of self-defeating beliefs can be uncovered in therapy which need to be tackled if progress is to be made. These beliefs include those associated with clients' presenting problem, core beliefs which may be uncovered later in therapy, low frustration tolerance (LFT) beliefs blocking the hard work necessary for change to occur, those that surface when setbacks are encountered, and those connected with crises such as suicidal feelings. Therefore you will need resilience and resourcefulness in tackling these clusters of irrational ideas as well as clinical acumen in uncovering the key beliefs that connect these clusters.

Learning to be persistent and creative in the disputing process can also be very difficult as it is easy to 'dry up' once the standard disputing questions have been asked: 'Is it logical?', 'Where's the evidence?' and 'Where is it going to get you?' When clients have not been 'persuaded' to surrender their irrational thinking by these questions, some therapists start to flounder and ask 'What do I do now?' Developing confidence and competence in disputing takes time but watching videos of leading REBTers, attending workshops, poring over therapy transcripts of Ellis, Dryden, DiGiuseppe, Hauck, Wolfe *et al.* can accelerate this learning process. One way to assess your disputing skills is how well you fare in debating with friends and colleagues. Can you defend your own viewpoint non-dogmatically as well as find flaws in your opponent's arguments?

What about the client who answers to the standard disputing questions 'No', 'There isn't any' and 'Nowhere apart from being unhappy' respectively? These replies are not signs that the client has eradicated his irrational ideas, but perhaps they appear less believable when discussing them in your office. However, this appearance is usually deceptive: the client probably has a lot of emotional investment in these ideas, maybe over a long period, and you need to discover what this investment is (e.g. the comfort of self-pity). Therefore do not take these replies at their face value but probe for the evidence that is located in the client's head, e.g. 'You say that this belief gets you nowhere apart from being unhappy' so why have you held on to it for the last ten years?'

Because you are practising rational emotive behaviour therapy does not automatically mean you are a rational thinker who will always be able to point out the inconsistencies in your clients' thinking (though some REBTers may think so). You are first and foremost a fallible human being who will, at times, make yourself disturbed about your clients' disturbances, e.g. 'I can't stand his incessant whining!' or agree with your clients' irrational thinking, e.g. 'She's right – you are worthless without a partner.' This latter disturbance is what Hauck (1966) calls 'the neurotic agreement in psychotherapy'. Before you can regain your clinical focus on the client's problems and teach him/her emotional problem-solving skills, you will need to engage in self-disputation, e.g. 'I can stand his incessant whining without liking it' and convince yourself that self-worth is not contingent upon having a partner or anything else in life.

Two of the criticisms levelled against REBT are that we put words into clients' mouths and we talk too much. When you are disputing, ask one question at a time and wait for a reply; do not overload clients with several questions all at once. Let your clients ponder the substance of the question in order to help them become more cognitively aware of the self-defeating nature of some of their beliefs. Try not to answer the question yourself; only do so if your client is really finding it difficult to come up with an answer. Phrase your answer tentatively and then put it back to the client for further reflection rather than triumphantly announcing the 'correct' reply. Asking too many questions and answering them yourself suggests you believe you have to make your client rational in the shortest time possible (or you have a problem with silences). This behaviour will probably produce clients who pay lip-service to rational ideas instead of genuinely endorsing them.

Disputing John's irrational beliefs

In this section, disputing is conducted by questioning the client's irrational belief and rational belief at the same time (traditionally in REBT, disputing of irrational and rational beliefs has been carried out consecutively). This procedure is known as structured disputing of clients' irrational and rational beliefs (Neenan and Dryden, 1999). We are not claiming that this is a superior form of disputing, just a different one. To make this process as clear as possible, write both beliefs and the disputing questions on a whiteboard. Clients can copy this on to a sheet of paper as well as the answers they provide (encourage clients to write down the best, i.e. most rational, answer rather than the first one that comes into their mind). Concurrent disputing usually examines first the premise (demand and preference) components of both beliefs and then moves on to their derivative components (in this case, self-depreciation and self-acceptance).

Michael: If we can recap, the irrational belief we are going to dispute is the one on the board 'I absolutely shouldn't have been rejected but as I was, this proves I'm unlovable.' Okay?

John: Yes, that's the culprit.

Michael: Now, what belief would you like to replace it with that's going to tackle your depression when you are rejected but will help you to continue asking women out?

John: Hmm. Well, something like 'I wish I hadn't been rejected, but I am not immune from rejection.'

Michael: What about your idea that you're unlovable?

John: Er ... 'I've been rejected but that doesn't mean I'm unlovable.'

Michael: What does it mean then ... ?

John: Er ... 'I can learn to accept myself irrespective of how others see or treat me.' I'm not supposed to believe this straightaway, am I?

Michael: This new or rational belief will take you some time to believe in and you might want to change it to make it more convincing as you gain more skill in disputing. It's difficult to come up with the right belief at the first attempt. Now I want to write this belief on the board also and deal with both beliefs in two parts. First of all, the demand versus the preference:

Demand	Preference
I absolutely shouldn't have been rejected	I really wish I hadn't been rejected but I am not immune from rejection

John: What happens now?

Michael: We are going to take a critical look at both beliefs to see which one stands up to inspection and which one doesn't. Okay?

John: Yes, I'm ready.

Michael: Which belief is sensible or logical and which one doesn't make sense or is illogical?

John:Er, um, that belief (pointing to the demand) is illogical, doesn't make sense but I'm not sure why.

Michael: Does it make sense to strongly prefer something not to have happened, like rejection, and then in the next breath to say therefore it absolutely shouldn't have happened?

John: Well, again, it doesn't make sense but I can't say any more than that. I don't think I really know too much about logic.

Michael: Okay, let's look at the next question: which belief is realistic and which one is unrealistic?

John: The demand is realistic because I didn't want to be rejected. Who does?

Michael: I'm sure most people would agree they didn't want to be rejected but there is a big difference between that understandable preference and demanding that it absolutely shouldn't have happened to you. You've got a demand and a preference in the same sentence. They can't both be true. Let's look at the demand first. Now if the universe strictly followed your demands, what would have never happened to you when you asked women out?

John: I'm not sure what you mean by 'if the universe strictly followed your demands'.

Michael: Let me give you an example: if I demanded that everyone must like me and the universe followed my demands as if it was my servant, would everyone like me?

John: Yes, they would. They wouldn't have any choice in it.

Michael: But is my belief realistic?

John: No, it isn't. The world doesn't work like that. People make up their own minds if they like you or not; you can't control people.

Michael: Now with your demand that you absolutely shouldn't have been rejected, is that a realistic belief?

John: No, it isn't realistic.

Michael: Why not?

John: Because I can't make the world or people do my bidding any more than you can. I have been rejected, no two ways about it.

Michael: In fact, we could say you should have been rejected. Do you know why we can say that?

John: You've lost me again.

Michael: (pointing to the window) Do you know why it should be raining?

John: Because it is. As we're talking it's raining outside.

Michael: Right. Now, should or should you not have been rejected?

John: I should have been rejected because I was.

Michael: Exactly. But instead of accepting this reality, without liking it of course, you've been demanding the opposite.

John: That's why I get so upset and stuck in life because I refuse to accept it. It seems so clear discussing it with you.

Michael: Practising it will be the hard part. Now let me ask you something else in relation to freedom of choice which you touched on earlier: if you shouldn't have been rejected, does this mean, in your mind, that women can only say 'yes' to you?

John: I suppose that's true but I never thought about it from their point of view. They had to say yes so I wouldn't have to suffer the pain of rejection.

Michael: Is it realistic then that you can deprive women of their freedom of choice?

John: (sighs) No.

Michael: And the evidence is ... ?

John: I have been rejected. I can't control their minds.

Michael: Let me ask you this: if you could control their minds, would you be a happy man?

John: I suppose I should say 'yes' but it wouldn't really help.

Michael: Why not?

John: Because I would never know if they really liked me. The doubt would eat away at me. (sighs) You know, this stuff I believe sounds so silly when we discuss it.

Michael: Clients often have this initial reaction because it's usually the first time their ideas have been brought out into the open and discussed in some depth. The fact that we're doing it now means that we've cleared the first hurdle and made some progress.

John: There's some hope for me after all then!

Michael: I certainly think so. Let's continue then. (pointing at the preference) Is that belief realistic?

John: Yes.

Michael: Why?

John: Because it supports my desire not to have been rejected but it accepts the reality that I was. I wish I could really believe that.

Michael: You can believe it if you work hard to make it part of your daily outlook on life. Also, when you believe it, you'll be less likely to disturb yourself when you are rejected again.

John: What do you mean 'again'?

Michael: Well, it's highly unlikely that women are going to start falling at your feet because you've spent time learning REBT. We teach realistic thinking, not positive or fantasy thinking.

John: (sighs) Yes, I know you're right.

Michael: Okay, let's move on. Which belief is more likely to be helpful in your life and why?

John: The preference. If I can learn to really believe it then I'm bound to ask more women out and increase my chances of striking lucky as well as learning to take rejection in my stride.

Michael: With the preference, do you think you will enjoy your relationships more?

John: I hope so. In the past I was always fearful of being dumped, so when I was actually going out with a woman I didn't enjoy it that much because I was expecting the chop at any time.

Michael: Anything unhelpful about the preference?

John: (laughs) Yes, I'll have to put these things into practice. That'll be a bit scary because I'll have to stop avoiding things.

Michael: So has the demand been helpful in some ways?

John: Well, as I've said before, it has kept me safe to some extent from more rejection and I can feel sorry for myself for not having a woman in my life. But all that is a dead-end because all it's kept me safe for is misery.

Michael: Moving on, which belief do you want to strengthen in your mind and act on?

John: Well, the demand has been dominating my thinking for a long time, so I want to get rid of it if I can. That's the one (pointing to the preference) that I want to strengthen in my mind and act on. Do you think I can?

Michael: You can if (emphasizes word) you put in the hard work to achieve these big changes in your life. You've got a lot to gain. How much longer do you want to continue with your present ways?

John: I don't.

Michael: Okay, we've finished for the moment part one of our examination, so let's now look at the derivative beliefs in part two.

Self-depreciation belief	Self-acceptance belief
As I have been rejected, this means I'm unlovable.	I have been rejected, but this does not mean I am unlovable. What it does mean is that I can learn to accept myself irrespective of how others see or treat me.

Michael: Now if we could use the same questions again for the derivative components of your beliefs. Now which belief is sensible or logical and which one doesn't make sense or is illogical?

John: The self-acceptance belief is sensible but I don't know why it's logical.

Michael: If a friend of yours was rejected would you agree with him if he condemned himself as unlovable?

John: No, I wouldn't.

Michael: Because ... ?

John: Because he's condemning himself over something like that and you can't put yourself on the scrap heap because of it. It's like condemning the whole of something on the basis of one of its parts.

Michael: Good. You've just told me why your belief is illogical and doesn't make sense.

John: My belief doesn't make sense, does it?

Michael: Doesn't make any sense to me either. Okay, which belief is unrealistic and which one is realistic?

John: I suppose that I'm not unlovable but I can't think why.

Michael: Well if you were truly unlovable, and the universe reflected that belief, how would people react to you?

John: They would all find me unlovable.

Michael: Past, present and future. Is that the reality of your life?

John: Of course not. My parents love me, and my brother and sister. I've got friends – they don't love me but you know what I mean.

Michael: And if you truly are unlovable then this or any other therapy won't be able to help you, will it?

John: No, because unlovable I am and unlovable I would stay.

Michael: So is your belief realistic?

John: No. Some people find me lovable, others don't, and some are not bothered either way.

Michael: You've just described how it probably is for most of us.

John: Why can't I think like this?

Michael: Because when we are emotionally disturbed we usually don't think clearly, and bad thinking habits can take hold very quickly and be very difficult to dislodge. Hence this examination of your thinking. Shall we move on?

John: Okay.

Michael: Which belief is helpful and which unhelpful?

John: Learning self-acceptance will be helpful.

Michael: In what way?

John: Because if I really believe it then I wouldn't be afraid of rejection or become depressed when it happens. But more importantly, I would have a very different image of myself. It would be great if I could feel confident around women.

Michael: Which brings us to the next question: which belief do you want to strengthen and act on?

John: Obviously the self-acceptance belief for the reasons I've just said. It won't happen overnight, will it?

Michael: The process of change doesn't usually work like that. We need to strengthen these rational beliefs over time and weaken your irrational beliefs over time. This disputing process goes on in therapy and in your daily life until you think, feel and act differently.

John:That's what I want.

The advantage of structured disputing is helping clients see more clearly that their irrational beliefs are illogical, unrealistic and unhelpful while their rational beliefs are logical, realistic and helpful because both beliefs are questioned together. A disadvantage of this approach is overwhelming clients by the simultaneous concentration on both beliefs and the accompanying questions. If this is the case, one question and one belief per session might be all that some clients can manage, e.g. focusing on a derivative belief to determine how realistic it is.

In structured disputing, it is important clients understand and agree with your arguments before moving them on to the next line of enquiry. However, if some clients are not persuaded by or interested in a particular argument, then you are advised to locate an argument that is more productive for them (in the above excerpt, John found realistic and pragmatic arguments the most stimulating). The aim of in-session structured disputing is to encourage clients to carry it out between sessions, so they eventually dispute irrational beliefs in their heads without the need of whiteboards or pieces of paper.

Intellectual insight and emotional insight

Once the initial phase of cognitive disputing has been completed, clients can usually see the potential for change if they adopt rational beliefs and give up irrational beliefs. This awareness is often referred to as clients arriving at intellectual insight into their problems as the benefits of an emerging rational outlook are only theoretical at this stage – this outlook has not yet been tested in those areas of clients' lives where they experience their emotional problems. When rational ideas are tested in such situations, they often prove to be weak and ineffective as they are quickly overwhelmed by the reactivation of powerful and long-standing irrational ideas. As Dryden (1995b) points out, clients may have integrated the rational solution to their problems into their knowledge systems, they have not yet integrated this solution into their belief systems.

When this latter form of integration has occurred, clients can be said to have arrived at emotional insight into their problems. This means that clients have been forcefully and consistently acting in support of their rational beliefs and disputing their irrational ones; consequently, they are now able to react to troublesome events without emotional disturbance and thereby employ a productive problem-solving focus.

This distinction between intellectual and emotional insight is also called the 'head–gut' split because clients often say 'I believe it up here (tapping head) but don't feel it down here (prodding stomach).' You can anticipate that clients will experience some difficulties in moving from intellectual to emotional insight by initiating a discussion on the subject; this acts as a prelude to considering ways to deepen clients' convictions in rational ideas and weaken their convictions in irrational ideas. For example, 'What do you think you'll need to do in order to get your new rational beliefs into your gut?' I discuss these issues with John:

Michael: Now you've agreed that you want to strengthen your rational beliefs and weaken your irrational ones. How do you think you go about this?

John: I suppose you try to think differently every day, that sort of thing.

Michael: Is thinking differently every day all that is required to bring about change?

John: I'm sure there are other things too but I'm not sure what you're getting at.

Michael: Okay. If I was unfit and wanted to run a marathon in nine months' time, would just thinking about it do the trick?

John: Of course not. You would have to train hard every day in all weathers if you wanted to be fit enough to complete the marathon in nine months' time.

Michael: So thinking about a situation in the right way is not enough. Do you see what I'm driving at?

John: Yes, I do. I've got to get out there and do it every day. Put into practice what we've been discussing in this room.

Michael: That's right. It's not only thinking differently but acting differently. Sometimes client say about their new rational beliefs that they believe them up here (tapping forehead) but not down here (prodding stomach) in their gut. To get those beliefs from the head to the gut takes a lot of hard work and persistence.

John: I bet it does, but it needs to be done if I want to make progress and stop living on my own and all those other things I want to change.

Michael: Now your irrational beliefs have had a powerful influence over the years on your thoughts, feelings and behaviours. Agreed?

John: Agreed, otherwise I would have been enjoying life like my brother.

Michael: Now these beliefs probably seem natural to you after holding them for so long.

John: That's true.

Michael: What will you need to do to make them unnatural to you and the rational beliefs natural to you?

John: Dispute them all the time and take on board the rational beliefs.

Michael: And act against the irrational beliefs and in support of your new rational beliefs. Will this process feel easy and comfortable?

John: Of course not. Actually, it's going to be quite scary doing the things I usually avoid.

Michael: Because it's scary doing these things, does that mean you won't be able to carry them out?

John: No, it just means I've got to work harder to see it through. I do want to see it through.

Michael: The 'it' being the changes you want.

John: Yes.

Michael: And to start putting ideas into practice to bring about these changes, we need to discuss your first homework assignment.

John: So what is it going to be then?

Michael: We'll come to that in a moment.

So far in this chapter, we have looked at cognitive disputing but as disputing in REBT is conducted on a multimodal basis, we now need to consider behavioural, emotive and imaginal methods of challenging irrational beliefs and internalizing rational beliefs.

Behavioural disputing

As we behave the way we think, this form of disputing involves clients acting against their irrational beliefs and engaging in behaviour that is congruent with their rational beliefs. For example, a man who believes he cannot tolerate standing in long queues is encouraged to do so not only to challenge behaviourally this idea but also to act in support of his new idea that 'I can stand it but I don't like it.' As Walen, DiGiuseppe and Dryden (1992, p. 169) point out, 'the RE[B]T practitioner will not be confident that the patient has internalised a new philosophy until it is reflected in behavioral change'. Behavioural tasks allow clients to practise *in vivo* their new rational ideas and develop emotional control.

Two major behavioural disputing strategies are stay-in-there assignments and risk-taking exercises (Grieger and Boyd, 1980). Stay-in-there assignments encourage clients to stay in unpleasant situations they usually avoid in order for them to overcome their disturbed feelings and behaviours about these situations, e.g. being in the same room as spiders, listening to long-winded colleagues without interrupting them, accepting criticism without automatically defending themselves. These assignments can be done implosively (i.e. fully and immediately) or gradually by increasing the degree of difficulty associated with each task. For example, a person with claustrophobia could stay in a small room until her disturbed feelings pass or, alternatively, spend increasing amounts of time in the room over several days or weeks until her fear dissipates.

Risk-taking exercises involve clients undertaking activities that might bring, among other outcomes, failure, poor results, disapproval or rejection. The risk is the uncertainty of outcome but nothing ventured, nothing gained or, in REBT terms, learning that risk-taking is an important step towards self-actualization (realizing one's potential). For example, a man who usually avoids public speaking because he might not give a perfect performance, finally 'takes the plunge' to prove to himself that doing the task is more important than doing it perfectly and to add another string to his professional bow.

Behavioural tasks are usually carried out as negotiated homework assignments but such tasks can also be carried out in-session. For example, a client who was putting off starting a college essay made no progress with homework tasks to overcome her procrastination; however, when she was asked to start writing the essay halfway through a counselling session the blocks were quickly identified and dealt with, which then provided her with the momentum to continue the essay outside of the session.

Sometimes novice REBTers assume that if behavioural change has occurred then there has been accompanying cognitive change, e.g. 'He's going out now and meeting more people so his thinking must have changed.' However, behavioural and cognitive change do not always keep in step. A client may be behaviourally exposed to a fear and learns to tolerate it yet remains cognitively stuck (i.e. still clinging to irrational beliefs). Leahy (1998, p. 350) asks 'what "behavioral exposure" really teaches the patient – what does it confirm or disconfirm? For example, if someone has a fear of flying and she flies 10 times, what does this "exposure" disconfirm if she is practicing safety-prayers or seeking reassurance?' From a cognitive perspective, behavioural exposure provides only partial exposure to an unpleasant activating event; full exposure occurs when clients' covert avoidance behaviours (e.g. distraction, thought stopping) are dropped and they learn to face and deal constructively with their worst-case scenarios. Whatever techniques you use to promote belief change, always return to an examination of clients' thinking to determine if a rational outlook is developing.

Imaginal disputing

This form of disputing uses mental images or pictures to challenge clients' irrational thinking. As McMullin (1986, p. 273) points out, 'since images do not involve language, clients can often shift their perceptions more rapidly and completely using visual images rather than semantics'. A major form of imaginal disputing is rational-emotive imagery, of which there are two versions (Maultsby, 1975; Maultsby and Ellis, 1974).

In the Ellis version, clients are asked to close their eyes and vividly imagine a troublesome situation where an unhealthy negative emotion occurs (anxiety about chairing a meeting). Clients are urged to experience the full force of their unhealthy negative emotion and then, without altering any details of the activating event, to change it to a healthy negative emotion (concern about chairing a meeting). Clients are asked to open their eyes and report how this affective shift was achieved. The ideal answer, of course, is that this shift occurred when clients replaced irrational ideas with rational ones.

In the Maultsby version, clients are asked to close their eyes and vividly imagine a troublesome situation where an unhealthy negative emotion occurs but, this time, repeat only rational ideas to themselves until a healthy negative emotion is experienced. Clients are then asked to open their eyes and reveal what rational ideas they used to achieve this.

It is important in both versions that feedback is obtained in order for you to determine if the imagery exercises were carried out in the prescribed fashion. Some clients might reveal that emotional change was achieved by distraction, making an unpleasant event more tolerable by changing some aspects of it, and adopting positive statements instead of rational ones, e.g. 'I was able to imagine accepting myself in that situation because I know that people really do like me even if they don't show it.' Grieger and Boyd (1980, p. 179) suggest that Ellis's version should be used 'during the working through process [i.e. adopting a rational outlook] because it facilitates cognitive disputation' and Maultsby's version 'for [rational-emotive] reeducation purposes because it is geared to the ingraining of rational ideas'.

Imagery can also be used as a form of preparation or mental rehearsal before clients carry out their *in vivo* behavioural tasks. In their mind's eye they can visualize themselves, first, coping adequately in a particular situation and then, secondly, performing inadequately in the same situation. Strategies are devised to deal with both outcomes. Only preparing clients for the first outcome can indicate to them that success is assured.

Emotive disputing

In this form of disputing, techniques are used which unleash or strongly arouse clients' disturbed emotions. This is achieved by encouraging your clients to dispute forcefully and energetically their disturbance-producing ideas. These techniques help clients to move from intellectual to emotional insight in tackling their problems. However, it is usually very difficult to influence or manipulate clients' emotions as can be done with their cognitions and behaviours. Therefore you need to remind your clients that 'emotional change often lingers behind behavioural and cognitive change ...' so that persisting with their cognitive-behavioural tasks may not bring them 'immediate or even intermediate affective benefit' (Dryden, 1995a, p. 43).

The most famous REBT emotive technique is known as a shame-attacking exercise (Ellis, 1969). This teaches clients to act in a 'shameful' way in real life in order to provoke disapproval or attract ridicule from others (e.g. taking an imaginary dog for a walk; asking directions to the local train station while standing outside of it). Simultaneously with this behavioural component of the exercise, clients are reminded to dispute vigorously their shame-inducing beliefs, e.g. 'Just because I'm acting stupidly does not make me a stupid person. I can accept myself no matter what others think of me.' Such exercises teach clients how they frequently overestimate the degree of opprobrium they believe they will incur from others and that it is not awful to behave stupidly or reveal a weakness.

Another emotive technique is authentic self-disclosure (Ellis and Knaus, 1977) whereby clients reveal to others genuine things about themselves that they would rather keep hidden (e.g. a man tells his 'I wouldn't be seen dead in counselling' friends that he is seeing a counsellor). By risking such self-disclosure, clients can learn to strive for greater self-acceptance as well as re-evaluate how shameful their perceived defects or weaknesses actually are.

In summary, we have examined multimodal disputing with particular emphasis on in-session cognitive disputing. In order to carry out *in vivo* disputing, the next step is to negotiate with your client a clinically relevant homework assignment which is the focus of the next chapter.

Chapter 4
Homework

In this chapter, we look at the clinical rationale for carrying out homework; types of homework tasks; troubleshooting any obstacles to carrying out the tasks; and the negotiation, content, execution and review of homework assignments.

Rationale for homework assignments

Homework has been an important feature of REBT since its inception in 1955 (Wessler and Wessler, 1980). If your client sees you for one hour every week, how is he/she going to use the other 167 hours before the next appointment? As Persons (1989, pp. 141–2) observes: 'Situations that arouse powerful affect probably involve the patient's key underlying ideas, and the ability to work on these when they are activated offers a potent opportunity for change that would be missed if all therapeutic work took place during therapy sessions.'

Homework is the activity carried out between sessions which puts into daily practice the learning that occurs in your office. Clients can claim that their irrational thinking is changing, but how is this to be verified unless they provide behavioural evidence of such change? For example, a client who states that it would no longer be awful if she gave wrong answers to questions asked by her lecturer still does not speak up when questions are asked by him. Has she really given up awfulizing about giving the wrong answers? We very much doubt it. Unless a rational philosophy is acted upon it is not going to bring about the changes that clients, desire; so what goes on outside of therapy sessions is ultimately more important than what goes on inside of them.

Homework tasks allow clients to develop confidence and competence in tackling their problems, thereby reducing the chances of a full-blown relapse; in addition, they are less likely to become dependent on you as the agent of change in their lives. Becoming a self-therapist is an important goal for clients in REBT; homework facilitates and accelerates clients' progress towards this goal. Burns (1989, p. 545) suggests 'that compliance with self-help assignments may be the most important predictor of thera- peutic success'. You can point this out to those clients who are reluctant to undertake such assignments.

The word 'homework' can prove troubling for some clients as it usually conjures up unpleasant memories of their schooldays, e.g. 'I hate that word. It always reminds me of my parents lecturing me to "do your homework or you'll become the class dunce". Do we have to use it?' Clients can use whatever term they choose or you can suggest alternative terms such as self-help tasks, between-session assignments, real-life activi- ties or problem-solving.

Types of homework tasks

These can be listed as cognitive, behavioural, imaginal and emotive (these categories were discussed in the previous chapter on disputing; additional techniques will be described here).

Cognitive tasks

These tasks help clients to become more informed about the theory and practice of REBT and thereby deepen their intellectual insight into their problems and the required methods to overcome them.

Reading

Encouraging clients to read REBT books, articles, pamphlets etc. is called bibliotherapy, i.e. reading as one means of promoting therapeutic change. There is a substantial body of REBT self-help literature which you can recommend to your clients: for example, *A Rational Counseling Primer* by Howard Young (1974), *A New Guide to Rational Living* by Albert Ellis and Robert Harper (1975), *Hold Your Head Up High* by Paul Hauck (1991a) and *10 Steps to Positive Living* by Windy Dryden (1994a). You should acquaint yourself with this literature if you want to suggest appropriate reading homework to your clients. Always ascertain if your clients have any reading difficulties and/or their level of interest in such assignments.

Listening

This can involve listening to tapes of REBT lectures on various aspects of its theory and practice, e.g. Albert Ellis speaking on *Assertiveness Training* (1979a) and *Unconditionally Accepting Yourself and Others* (1986); Ray DiGiuseppe discussing *What Do I Do With My Anger: Hold It In or Let It*

Out? (1989). These tapes can be obtained from the Albert Ellis Institute for Rational Emotive Behavior Therapy (see appendix for address). Clients can also listen to relaxation tapes as an adjunct to cognitive restructuring of their anxiogenic thinking.

REBT favours clients tape recording their sessions in order for them to reflect on the session content away from your office. Listening to such tapes between sessions often brings greater understanding of important therapeutic points made in the sessions. Clients may process information inadequately in your sessions because, among other reasons, they are emotionally disturbed or they may be reluctant to admit they do not understand the points you are making. On their own, clients are likely to feel less inhibited or distracted and thereby more able to focus on the session tape and bring their comments about it to the next session.

If some clients have strong adverse reactions to hearing their voices on tape (e.g. 'I can't believe I'm talking so much rubbish' or 'I come across as so stupid on the tape'), these reactions can be cognitively processed to produce a favourable response to session taping (e.g. 'If it is rubbish I'd better listen to the tapes to help me understand why I believed it for so long'; 'I'm only stupid because I label myself that way. Listening to the tapes without the name-calling would be more productive'); however, if some clients are insistent that the taping should stop, then comply with their requests.

Writing

A formal method of challenging irrational beliefs is by encouraging clients to guide themselves through the ABCDE model by asking a series of questions which they can write down. An example of a self-help form is:

A = What am I most disturbed about?
B = What is my irrational belief?
C = What is my unhealthy negative emotion?
D = What is a different way to think about the situation through disputing my irrational belief?
E = What are my new thoughts, feelings and behaviours about the situation?

This example of cognitive homework is given to clients only after they have gained proficiency in the use of such self-help forms through in-session practice.

Other writing tasks include essays where clients can learn to explore rational ideas, e.g. a client who keeps demanding that he should not have lost his job two years ago is asked to write a composition entitled 'Why I should have lost my job two years ago.' Keeping diaries can also be suggested whereby important thoughts and feelings can be noted and the situations in which they occur, e.g. a client becomes more aware of the stressful situations that trigger alcohol-related beliefs such as 'I can't stand these long meetings. I need a drink to calm down once they're finished.'

Behavioural tasks

These tasks are a key feature of homework as clients learn to act against their disturbed thoughts and feelings and act in ways that foster rational ideas and non-disturbed feelings. Therefore engaging in *in vivo* tasks is a behavioural means to achieve a cognitive end (i.e. philosophical restructuring). For example, a person who only speaks at meetings after others have done so in order not to say something 'that might not be liked' is encouraged to speak first to counter her needs for approval and learn to be more independently minded. Behavioural tasks are the primary means of achieving emotional insight because clients may doubt the efficacy of their new rational beliefs if they are not acted upon.

Imagery tasks

By using mental images or pictures clients can learn to modify or change their disturbed emotional reactions to situations. Rational-emotive imagery is the major technique in this respect (see previous chapter). Once clients have been taught an imagery procedure, such as mentally rehearsing a new behaviour, they can practise it on a daily basis before entering the actual situation (e.g. being assertive with rude colleagues). Clients can also learn to habituate themselves to feared events by imaginally and repeatedly confronting these events so they can constructively deal with them if they occur (e.g. a client who does not get his longed-for promotion views it as unfortunate but not awful and thereby is still able to gain satisfaction in his present position.)

A technique which helps clients to commit themselves to change is inaction v. action imagery (Neenan and Palmer, 1998): clients are encouraged to visualize as graphically as possible the consequences of not tackling their problems (e.g. stuck in a dead-end job; poor social opportunities); then to visualize as vividly as possible taking decisive action (e.g. applying for interesting jobs; seeking exciting social opportunities). This task can be done several times daily and over the next few weeks the inaction imagery can be faded out. If some clients have difficulties in creating images associated with problem-solving, exercises can be used to improve their image-building capabilities (Lazarus, 1984).

Emotive tasks

These tasks are designed to engage fully clients' disturbed emotions in order to change or ameliorate them through persistent and forceful disputing of their ingrained irrational ideas. Besides those exercises described in Chapter 3, others include devising passionate rational self-statements and engaging in forceful self-dialogues. Passionate rational self-statements consist of vigorous, dramatic self-verbalizations aimed at uprooting self-defeating thinking, e.g. 'No matter how much I want the approval of others, I damned well don't need it! Tough shit if people turn their backs on me.' As Yankura and Dryden (1994, p. 2) observe: 'The emotions we experience are ... influenced by the manner in which we talk to ourselves.'

Forceful self-dialogues encourage clients to use their rational voices to argue vehemently against their irrational voices so that the latter are eventually silenced (or at least made much less audible). Such dialogues can be tape recorded in-session (usually of several minutes duration) and clients can listen to them between sessions as a means of strengthening their commitment to emerging rational ideas (Ellis *et al.*, 1988). An example of a forceful self-dialogue is a client with chronic alcohol problems:

Irrational voice: One last binge this weekend on the booze and then I'll give it up for good.

Rational voice: Crap! You mean another binge on self-deception.

Irrational voice: No, no. I really mean it this time. My wife is threatening to leave me.

Rational voice: Bollocks! Not that old record again. You said the same thing with your last wife but you didn't give up the booze and she left you. The same thing happened with all the girlfriends you made the pledge to. The only pledge you believe in is not keeping to any you make.

Irrational voice: Yeah, but it will be different this time – I've hit rock bottom. My life is a complete mess.

Rational voice: That rock bottom garbage has as much credibility as your pledges. Underneath your supposed rock bottom is always another one. You'll either get to the centre of the earth or die in the attempt.

Irrational voice: What else can I do then?

Rational voice: There's only one realistic option left and you know what it is: an alcohol rehabilitation centre.

Irrational voice: I know people who've been to rehab. and it didn't work for them.

Rational voice: How very comforting for you! They usually left the rehab. once the hard work started and drifted back into your circle. You have other friends who went to rehab., finished the programme and you've never seen them since. Why? Because they're clean now and don't want to mix with you any more.

Irrational voice: Well, I'll think about it. Maybe it might work for me.

Rational voice: Don't think about it – do it! Contact the alcohol team today. Give up all the excuses and bullshit and then, only then, you might have a real chance of not seeing life through a bottle.

Emotive methods are not used to ventilate feelings as this usually produces respite from, but not removal of, unhealthy negative emotions – but to effect a philosophical change in an individual's outlook.

Negotiating homework tasks

Though it might seem obvious, negotiation is about discussion and compromise. In our experience, therapists often fall into the trap of telling clients what their homework tasks should be for some of the following reasons: 'teacher knows best', clients are too slow or hesitant in making up their mind about what to do, therapists want clients 'to feel good about themselves' as quickly as possible, therapists' goals for client change are more ambitious than clients' goals for change, therapists have to prove their clinical competence by forcing the pace of change.

Telling clients what their assignments will be often leads to understandable resistance on their part or compliance in your office but non-compliance and inaction outside of it. If you monitor your clients' non-verbal reactions (e.g. jaw tightening, gazing into the middle distance) and/or para-verbal responses (e.g. a string of hmms), these will usually indicate whether or not your clients agree with your suggestions. So ensure that your clients are active participants in homework negotiation.

Negotiating homework tasks using the criterion challenging, but not overwhelming (Dryden, 1995b)

In Chapter 3 we discussed behavioural disputing using implosive (flooding) or gradual methods. Flooding involves clients facing their fears fully and immediately while gradual desensitization takes clients through a hierarchy of progressively difficult tasks towards their ultimate fear. REBT argues that this gradualist philosophy in homework activities can actually strengthen some clients' low frustration tolerance (LFT) ideas, e.g. 'I have to go slowly in dealing with my anxiety as I can't stand much pressure' (this attitude can be construed as a need for comfort in carrying out unpleasant tasks; if constructive change is to be achieved it requires clients to develop a philosophy of effort and give up their comfort needs). Such beliefs can make therapy a protracted experience and convince some clients that their LFT is too much to bear and thereby terminate therapy before significant change is achieved. Ellis (quoted in Dryden, 1991b, p. 36) asserts that clients 'who are willing to act against their phobias implosively, overcome them much more quickly, and as far as I can see much more thoroughly'.

However, in our clinical experience, few clients choose flooding methods while we tend to discourage gradual ones because of their potential for iatrogenic consequences, i.e. therapy making their existing problems worse. A middle way between total and graded exposure is negotiation based upon the principle of challenging, but not overwhelming, i.e. assignments that are sufficiently stimulating to promote therapeutic change but not so daunting that they may inhibit clients from carrying them out. Here is an example of such a negotiation:

Therapist: We've discussed your attitude towards clearing out that spare room which you've avoided doing for many months.

Client: I told you why – it's so bloody boring!

Therapist: But you want to get it done, you said, and stop putting it off.

Client: That's right. That room desperately needs doing.

Therapist: Now you could get that room cleared out in one day through a maximum effort on your part and it's all finished.

Client: You must be joking. I'm definitely not doing that.

Therapist: What's your suggestion?

Client: Well, I think fifteen minutes would be reasonable. I can't see anything wrong with that.

Therapist: Why only fifteen minutes?

Client: Any longer than that and I'm going to get really bored and very angry.

Therapist: The problem with fifteen minutes is that it's actually going to reinforce your low frustration tolerance for carrying out boring tasks because you're going to keep telling yourself 'I can't stand it!' You really need to work through the anger and put up with the boredom and then, when you're less disturbed about the task, stop doing it.

Client: That might take a couple of hours!

Therapist: You are more likely to learn in those few hours that you can tolerate doing boring tasks but without liking them. I doubt if you'll learn anything new in those fifteen minutes and you'll probably take as long cleaning out the room as you did avoiding it.

Client: It makes sense what you say. I suppose it will make an interesting experiment and I expect I'll survive it.

Therapist: So have you agreed then to clear out the spare room for a sustained period of two hours?

Client: Yes. I'll do it this Sunday afternoon.

In the above extract, the client was obviously not interested in making a 'maximum effort' to conquer his LFT regarding clearing out the spare room; his own suggestion of fifteen minutes did not carry, from the REBT viewpoint, the potential for the development of new attitudes to attack his LFT. Such attitudes would be more likely to emerge through the client's prolonged immersion in an aversive situation he believes he cannot tolerate.

'Win–win' formula of homework tasks

This means that whatever happens with homework assignments, clients are bound to learn some therapeutic points:

1. The agreed homework task is successfully completed. How did the client manage to do this? (By committing herself to the hard work required to achieve her goals.)
2. The agreed homework task was not only completed successfully but the client also carried out additional, even more difficult tasks. What lies behind such seemingly commendable enthusiasm? (The client might be a perfectionist who sees problem-solving in all-or-nothing terms.)
3. The client did a homework task but not the one agreed with the therapist. Why did the client not keep to the agreed task? (The agreed task was too difficult but the client may have been afraid to tell the therapist for fear of losing her approval.)
4. The agreed homework task was attempted but quickly abandoned. What went wrong? (The client may have abysmal low frustration tolerance.)

5. The agreed homework task was not carried out. What prevented the client from carrying it out? (The clinical rationale for homework may not have been clearly conveyed or homework setting was conducted too quickly thereby leaving the client unsure about the precise details of the task.)
6. The client continually agrees to carry out tasks but never does. Why does the client say 'Yes' when she really means 'No'? (The client might be displaying passive–aggressive characteristics.)
7. The client refuses to even consider the idea of homework. What is going on here? (The client might believe, 'I'm paying you to help me, not do the bloody work for you!')

Whatever happens with the above homework scenarios, each will provide grist for the cognitive mill: namely, that information can be gathered by you to determine what are the spurs or blocks to task completion. Even though we have described homework as a 'win–win' formula, in reality, if some clients make only half-hearted attempts to or never carry out their homework tasks little, if any, lasting progress will be made. This is an important point for your clients to understand.

Is the task relevant to what was discussed or done in the session?

This might seem obvious but in our experience some therapists, usually novice ones, negotiate tasks that have no connection with the preceding session. For example, a client with spider phobia, instead of being asked to read books on or watch videos of spiders as part of a desensitization programme, is asked to write an essay entitled 'Is there anything wrong with being anxious?' The client might be bewildered by such a task but go along with it because 'I'm sure the therapist knows what he's doing even if I don't.' If your clients cannot see, explain or agree with the session–homework task link you have suggested, then think again about the relevance of the proposed assignment.

Even though your clients have agreed to carry out the tasks, do they have sufficient skills to make task-completion more likely? For example, if a client's social skills have decayed through years of chronic problems, it is highly unrealistic for her to be asked to attend a party as a first homework task. Social skills training and in-session rehearsal of such skills would be sorely needed before the client got anywhere near a party. So skills assessment is another task you need to undertake as part of homework negotiation.

Trying versus doing

When you ask clients if they will carry out their homework assignments, a common reply is: 'I'll try.' While this reply usually indicates that these clients will make an effort, it also denotes a lack of commitment on their part because they have not yet grasped the philosophical implications of what real change actually requires from them – persistent and forceful action. You can point out to them that they may have been trying for years to overcome their problems but success has eluded them because there was no real commitment to carrying through a programme of work. So do they want to continue in therapy with the same attitude that has been unproductive in their lives so far?

If they want to acquire a constructive problem-solving outlook, then they need to start doing tasks and give up trying to do them.

You can communicate to your clients the difference between trying and doing by asking them for example: 'When this session is finished will you try to leave this room, which means you won't get out of the door, or will you actually do it? Did you try to drive to the session, which means you wouldn't have got here, or did you drive the car here?' Clients usually grasp this distinction quickly but do not expect them to put it into immediate effect!

When, where and how often?

When a client says 'I'll do the homework probably next week', this frequently means she will not carry out the negotiated task or it is not a priority for her but to be 'fitted in' if she remembers to do it and nothing more interesting intervenes. In order to concentrate clients' minds on carrying out the tasks, ask the following questions: when will you carry out the task? where will you do it? and how often will you do it? Specificity, not vagueness, should guide homework negotiation and thereby makes it more likely that clients will commit themselves to executing their assignments.

Troubleshooting obstacles to undertaking homework assignments

Once your clients have understood and agreed with the clinical rationale for carrying out their homework tasks and have stated when, where and how often they are going to do them, the next step is to discuss any potential or actual blocks to homework completion. Blocks are not only identified but also methods are discussed for overcoming them. For example, a client says she might forget to ring her in-laws to arrange a visit she has been dreading. Solution: leave a Post-it note on the telephone to remind herself. She then replies that the children might remove it, so another suggestion might be to keep the Post-it note in her purse instead. These excuses can seem trivial but they usually reflect deeper worries such as the acute discomfort clients will experience when they finally enter a previously avoided aversive situation.

These underlying issues need to be addressed if homework is to be undertaken, e.g. 'If you want to make yourself relatively comfortable in these situations you have to make yourself uncomfortable first. Unpleasant, but necessary, I'm afraid.' If clients cannot identify any blocks to homework completion, you can suggest some on the basis of your clinical experience, e.g. 'Clients often say they will have difficulty in finding the time to do these tasks, will you have trouble finding the time?'

Rewards and penalties

These are used as part of homework negotiation in order to encourage your clients to carry out their agreed tasks. Rewards can be anything that your clients enjoy and are not harmful to them or others. Clients reward themselves *after* they have carried out their tasks and the rewards should be proportionate to the time spent and degree of difficulty involved in carrying them out, e.g. a ten-minute imagery task is rewarded with a slice of cake rather than a trip to the theatre. Penalties (not punishments) are self-administered for not carrying out agreed tasks. The penalty is devised by the client and is usually an unpleasant one, e.g. not watching a favourite television programme, talking to someone 'who bores me to death'. Grieger and Boyd (1980, p. 145) suggest that rewards and penalties 'often provides the extra incentive that makes the difference between avoiding and completing it [homework]'.

However, the principle of rewards and penalties should be employed with caution as it

> can usually only be used with highly motivated clients. If your client seems to be struggling with just getting to therapy sessions, let alone completing assignments outside of therapy, then this intervention may not be appropriate for her. In fact, it may just contribute to an overall sense of failure if used with certain clients (Ellis and MacLaren, 1998, p. 93).

Do not rush homework negotiation

We hope that we have made clear that homework is a vital part of REBT and not an optional extra depending on the time available at the end of a session. Therefore it is important that you make provision for homework negotiation in the structure of the session – ten minutes or even longer for novice REBTers. If a clinically suitable homework task has emerged earlier in therapy and has been agreed upon, then obviously you will need less time at the end the session to discuss it again. Always ensure that you give your clients a written copy of the homework task to remind them what they have agreed to do. If the task is just verbally agreed, this opens the way for arguments in the next session over what was precisely discussed, e.g.:

Therapist: We agreed that you were to do the task twice daily.

Client: No, the way I remember it was to do the task every two days.

Negotiating John's homework task

In the last chapter, John's irrational belief and rational belief were disputed at the same time in order for him to start weakening his adherence to the former and begin strengthening his attachment to the latter. A homework task now needs to be agreed upon that follows logically from the work done in the session:

Michael: Based upon what we've done so far, what do you think might be an appropriate task for you to carry out in the next week?

John: Well, I'm not asking any women out straightaway just to suffer rejection so I can learn to put up with it.

Michael: Okay, that's what you won't do but what task will you do?

John: I'll start my diet.

Michael: Good, but in terms of the beliefs we've disputed in this session, what might help you to promote further learning?

John: I'm not sure.

Michael: Well, you said earlier that you wanted a very different image of yourself so you could feel confident around women. Remember?

John: Yes, I did say that.

Michael: That confidence is likely to result from acquiring self-acceptance in the face of rejection.

John: I want to learn that but, as I said, I'm not jumping in at the deep end straightaway.

Michael: Would it be helpful to read an REBT book on self-acceptance which will also help you to learn more about REBT?

John: I like reading so that will be a good start for me. What do you suggest?

Michael: *How to Develop Self-Acceptance* by Windy Dryden. It's an easy-to-read self-help book, about one hundred pages. You can order it from the local bookshop. How much of it do you think you will read before our next session?

John: A few pages or so, I expect.

Michael: It doesn't sound as if you are going to put much effort into this task. If you want change to be deep and enduring then you will need to work hard both in and out of therapy. If you don't put much in, you won't get much out.

John: That makes sense. I am rather lazy at times. Okay, I'll read twenty pages each day when I get the book.

Michael: And we can discuss your reaction to the book in the next session. Do you think there will be anything that prevents you from buying the book or reading twenty pages every day?

John: I've got the money to buy the book, so there won't be a problem there. What if the book's boring?

Michael: Well, you won't know that until you start reading it. But let's say it is boring, might there be good reasons to persist with it?

John: You've recommended it, it's about self-acceptance which I said I want to learn about, and I probably give up too quickly anyway.

Michael: Good. Now if the book is hard going, can you read five or ten pages at a time rather than twenty pages all in one go?

John: Yes, I can certainly do that.

Michael: In REBT, we sometimes like to suggest rewards for doing the task and penalties for not doing it. Would that help you?

John: Let's see if it does. I like to smoke one small cigar every day, so I can do that after the reading.

Michael: The reading being all twenty pages, not just five or ten pages. Okay?

John: Okay.

Michael: And the penalty?

John: Cleaning the house.

Michael: So what will that mean if you avoid the reading on any given day?

John: One hour of house cleaning. Ugh!

Michael: You can avoid that if you do the reading. Now as you can see I have been writing down the homework task on this form – which I will give you a copy of – so there will be no confusion or disagreement in the next session about the homework task discussed in this one. Any final questions before the session ends?

John: You're going to work me hard, aren't you.

Michael: Yes. You need to work hard if you want to bring about real and lasting change in your life. There's no other way.

John: A sobering thought to end on.

Homework assignments are usually negotiated at the end of a session and are reviewed at the beginning of the next one. With regard to a typical session agenda, homework usually provides the first and last items for discussion.

Reviewing homework assignments

At the beginning of every session ask your clients about their homework assignments (unless, of course, a crisis has emerged which needs to be dealt with immediately and therefore normal agenda setting has to be suspended). If you overlook this issue or enquire in a cursory or indifferent manner, you are communicating to your clients the unimportance of homework, so do not be surprised if clients lose interest in carrying out homework tasks. If they have carried out the agreed task, congratulate them and ask how they accomplished it and what they have learned from it. If they did not carry out the task, make sure you find out the reasons why, even if the client is reluctant to tell you:

Therapist: When you shrugged your shoulders about not doing the homework, what does that mean?

Client: I don't know (shrugs her shoulders again). I just didn't do it.

Therapist: Do you think it will be helpful to find out why you didn't do the task as this will provide more information about your problems?

Client: If you want.

Therapist: Was it lack of time, you couldn't be bothered, the task was too difficult ... ?

Client: I couldn't be bothered.

Therapist: Why was that?

Client: I'm not sure what I want from therapy, so I can't see the sense of doing any homework yet.

Therapist: That might be my fault in not having clarified what you want to achieve from therapy. If we can be really clear about your goals and the specific steps needed to achieve them, would you be ready to carry out some homework tasks?

Client: If I know where I'm going, then I will do the tasks. I'm feeling a bit better about them already.

If clients do not carry out their agreed tasks, your own emotional reactions might need to be monitored. For example, you might get angry because you believe that your clients absolutely should work hard in therapy or feel anxious that continuing non-compliance from them will prove that you are an incompetent therapist. Obviously you will need to challenge and change your own disturbance-producing ideas before you can regain your clinical focus on clients' blocks to homework completion.

'Doing the homework is critical for the therapeutic process to be effective' (Walen, DiGiuseppe and Dryden, 1992, p. 272). Homework is the means by which clients move from intellectual to emotional insight into their problems and thereby internalize a rational philosophy of living. How this is accomplished is the subject of the next chapter.

Chapter 5
Working Through

In this chapter, we examine those features of therapy which comprise the working-through phase of REBT. These features include multimodal disputing of an irrational belief, teaching the non-linear model of change, becoming a self-therapist, using force and energy in effecting behavioural change, uncovering core beliefs, choosing between philosophical and non-philosophical change, removing obstacles to change and teaching relapse prevention.

Introduction

> Rational-emotive [behavioural] working through constitutes the heart of RE[B]T. Helping clients work through their problems – that is, systematically giving up their irrational ideas – is where most of the therapist's energy and time are directed and where longlasting change takes place. Successful working through leads to significant change, whereas unsuccessful working through leads to no gain or to superficial gain at best. It is as simple as that (Grieger and Boyd, 1980, p. 122).

Your clients are unlikely to experience enduring change in their lives unless they repeatedly and forcefully dispute their irrational beliefs in a variety of aversive situations. With regard to disputing, Hauck (1980, p. 244) states that

> in all counseling, one task is more critical than any other. It is self-debate. Throughout your counseling it is practically always critical that you keep the client oriented toward questioning, challenging, and debating with himself over his irrational ideas ... debate, debate, debate.

Such disputing (D) leads to the weakening of clients' disturbance-producing thinking and the strengthening of their rational or disturbance-reducing beliefs to achieve new effects (E) in thoughts, feelings and behaviours. Grieger (1991) states that REBT working through is a 24 hours a day and seven days a week endeavour. While this statement is extreme, it does point to the importance of clients continuing to work on themselves regularly, over time. Methods facilitating the working through process will now be described.

Suggest different homework tasks to dispute the same irrational belief

REBT theory hypothesizes that thoughts, feelings and behaviours are interdependent and interactive processes: namely, that thoughts will contain emotional and behavioural components; feelings and behaviours will each have elements of the other two. Therefore the preferred and possibly optimal way of attacking an irrational belief and generating a rational alternative is through several modalities: cognitive, emotive, imaginal and behavioural. Such a multimodal approach can help to keep clients interested in the change process as well as having their problems addressed on a number of different levels. For example, a client who enjoys and usually suggests reading assignments (cognitive) as a means of challenging his irrational thinking is encouraged to experiment with other techniques and modalities to deepen and accelerate the process of change:

Client: What for? I enjoy reading very much. It's opening up different viewpoints on my problems. I feel more relaxed in groups now.

Therapist: But are you speaking up in the groups? Your problem was saying something silly and looking a fool in the group.

Client: I speak up a little bit more, so I'm making progress.

Therapist: That's good, but are you ever the first to speak up?

Client: No. I haven't got that far yet.

Therapist: What holds you back?

Client: Still the fear of looking silly. I haven't been able to reason it out of my head yet.

Therapist: So how far has the reading helped you deal with that?

Client: Not that much, I suppose.

Therapist: The trouble with using only one technique or just a couple of them is that it is a very narrow way of advancing personal change. What happens if they don't help you deal effectively with your problems?

Client: Hmm. You don't make much progress which I suppose, in all truthfulness, I'm not doing as well as I would like.

Therapist: Okay. I'm not asking you to abandon reading but try other things as well.

Client: Such as ...?

Therapist: You could be very bold and take the risk of speaking up first in the group or deliberately say something stupid in order to both accept yourself and compare the actual reaction of the group with the one you fear. How would these tasks help in addition to the reading?

Client: Well, if I actually did them I could make faster progress rather than the small steps I'm actually taking. The big change would be actually believing in my gut that I can say foolish things without putting myself down and give up this pathetic need for other people's approval.

Therapist: It's the action assignments that are going to bring about the changes you desire. Just reading about what is required of you without any accompanying action is rarely successful. Do you want to experiment with other techniques then, to see if you can make faster and deeper progress?

Client: Yes. I definitely see the sense in it.

Discuss the non-linear model of change

Some clients might imagine that change, once initiated, is a relatively smooth and uneventful process. Acknowledging the helpfulness of rational ideas in your office leads naturally to acting on them in the real world. In order to disabuse these clients of such ideas and prepare them for the vicissitudes of the change process, you can explain to them the non-linear model of change. This model shows clients they will experience varying degrees of success in disputing their irrational beliefs in relevant contexts as well as encountering setbacks in tackling their problems. As these setbacks and relapses can be anticipated, strategies can be devised to deal with them if and when they occur.

Change in REBT involves clients becoming less emotionally disturbed but not undisturbable (e.g. 'My anxiety has greatly diminished but not completely gone'); so change involves relative measures of success rather than absolute ones. Change can be measured along the following three major dimensions:

1. Frequency – are unhealthy negative emotions and self-defeating behaviours experienced less frequently than before?

2. Intensity – when unhealthy negative emotions and self-defeating behaviours are experienced, are they less intense than before?
3. Duration – do unhealthy negative emotions and self-defeating behaviours last for shorter periods than before?

Encourage your clients to keep a log of their unhealthy negative emotions and self-defeating behaviours and the situations in which they occur, so they can monitor emotional and behavioural change using these three dimensions. Sometimes clients can become disillusioned because of their perceived lack of progress in feeling less disturbed and acting in more constructive ways (e.g. 'I just feel the same – depressed and withdrawn'), but a log enables them to pinpoint affective and behavioural shifts that are more gradual, or even subtle, than dramatic and thereby helps them to realize that improvement is occurring. Also, recommend to your clients Albert Ellis's (1984) pamphlet, *How To Maintain and Enhance Your Rational-Emotive Therapy Gains*, which encapsulates many of the key points of the working through process.

Encourage clients to become their own therapists

The ultimate aim of REBT therapists is to make themselves redundant as clients increasingly take on the role of self-therapists. This role requires clients to take more responsibility for designing and executing their homework tasks, using the ABCDE model to conceptualize and tackle their emotional problems and selecting techniques to promote therapeutic change. As Dryden (1994b, p. 35) observes: 'Unless your clients can apply what they have learnt in therapy to their own lives at their own prompting, then whatever gains they may have achieved from therapy will probably not be maintained in the long run.'

If clients are successful in taking on this role, you will notice a corresponding decrease in your own level of activity (e.g. clients setting the agenda, uncovering their dogmatic musts and shoulds, making connections between their problems) which can then allow you to reconceptualize your role as a consultant, coach, mentor or adviser rather than as a therapist. The client as self-therapist should extend well beyond therapy and, if possible, be lifelong.

To encourage your clients to be more active in the problem-solving process, use less didactic teaching and more Socratic questioning as a means of promoting independent thinking and reducing dependence on your problem-solving abilities. Short, probing questions can help your clients to work through the ABCDE model:

- 'What happened at A?'
- 'How did you feel (or act) at C?'
- 'What were you telling yourself at B to feel (or act) that way at C?'
- 'What disputes (D) did you use to tackle that belief?'
- 'Can you think of a relevant homework task to challenge that belief?'
- 'What rational belief would you like to hold?'
- 'If you really internalize that rational belief, what new thoughts, feelings and behaviours (E) might it lead to?'

Of course, not all of your clients will be able to become self-therapists in the way described above; so do not automatically expect them to fulfil this role. Some clients will have great difficulty in attaining a small measure of change, let alone maintaining it. Therefore, whatever self-help abilities these clients do have, make the best use of them in therapy, e.g. a client who believes that jumping to conclusions is the heart of her problem is encouraged to write on a card 'Walk towards the conclusion, don't jump to it' to remind herself to consider carefully her facts before making a judgement.

Using force and energy to dispute irrational beliefs

Clients frequently adhere to their irrational beliefs with tremendous tenacity despite the accumulated evidence that these beliefs maintain their problems, e.g. 'I know that my perfectionist beliefs place unbearable strain on me but I'm afraid to give them up as I fear my high standards will drop alarmingly if I do.' Ellis (1979b) has urged REBTers to employ force and energy in disputing clients' irrational beliefs and, through such modelling, for clients to use vigour in self-disputation. Clients who challenge their disturbance-producing beliefs in a tepid and tentative manner are unlikely to make much of a dent in their irrational thinking, let alone dislodge it, e.g. 'Yes, I suppose I can just see that it wouldn't be awful if my son stopped talking to me. Hmm.' Such disputing may provide some measure of intellectual insight into clients' problems but lacks the vigour and drive needed to reach emotional insight into or a rational solution to the problem, e.g. 'If my son has stopped talking to me, too bad! His behaviour is a pain in my backside but certainly not the end of my world.'

If some clients have objections to using force and energy in tackling their problems (e.g. 'It seems a rather vulgar and loudmouthed way to be carrying on'), you can encourage them to suggest their own modifications to vigorous disputing which will suit their temperament, culture or age, e.g. an elderly client decides that 'quiet determination' is the way he wants to tackle his problems, not 'rushing about, shouting and screaming'. With regard to elderly clients, Ellis (1999, p. 12) shows them 'how to vigorously and powerfully change their self-defeating thoughts and feelings to firmly held self-helping cognitions and emotions'. However, in my (MN) experience on the other side of the Atlantic, elderly clients usually engage in rather more gentle questioning of their irrational ideas as they often lack the energy and inclination to do otherwise.

Extend situation-specific irrational beliefs to core beliefs

Clients usually subscribe to irrational beliefs at both specific and general levels. A situation-specific belief might be a wife's demand that her husband must take her out to dinner once a week otherwise this means that he does not love her. A core irrational belief can be seen as a very general form of some of the specific beliefs that your clients adhere to. With regard to the above example, a variety of situations are analysed where the woman makes demands on others (e.g. her son, friends, work colleagues) in order to prove she is loved/approved of: 'Others must give me what I demand because if they refuse, this will prove I'm worthless.' Tackling a core belief will deal with a number of situations simultaneously while challenging situation-specific beliefs are obviously more limited in scope. Thus, in the above example, her husband's refusal to comply with her demand is no longer met with anger and hurt while her core belief which underpins many situations no longer generates disturbance because she now embraces unconditional self-worth.

Dryden and Yankura (1995) suggest some guidelines for helping you to identify, challenge and change clients' irrational beliefs:

1. Look for common themes.

As problematic situations are discussed in therapy, common themes usually emerge that link these situations. For example, a man who procrastinates over a career change, stays in a relationship he is bored with, goes to the same destination every year for his holiday and pursues hobbies that no longer excite him may believe 'I must be absolutely certain that if I change things in my life they must work out well for me otherwise it will be awful if they don't.' You can present your hypotheses regarding core beliefs to clients for their consideration (remember that a hypothesis is open to disconfirmation, so do not present yours as if it was an established fact). It is unlikely that all of your clients' problems will be directly attributable to a single core belief. In our experience, it is typically two or three core beliefs that underlie clients' problems and involve both ego and discomfort disturbances.

2. Encourage clients to identify their own core irrational beliefs.

Point out to your clients that there might be a common theme running through their problems and can they identify it. Dryden and Yankura (1995, p. 57) suggest that 'prompting your client to do this sort of thinking on her own can help to prepare her for identifying core irrational beliefs on an independent basis after formal counselling has ended'.

3. Encourage clients to engage in self-observation.

When clients detect a core belief that connects a number of problems they are working on, ask them if they can pinpoint other and as yet undiscussed problem areas in their lives where this belief might be operative. Such detective work can help clients to improve considerably their cognitive awareness of the adverse impact of an irrational belief on many areas of their lives. Be cautious with this self-observation exercise as some clients who are struggling to cope with current problems may feel overwhelmed, and even terminate therapy, at the seemingly limitless number of problems rearing up before them.

4. Help clients to design a core rational philosophy.

If your clients have uncovered a core irrational philosophy (e.g. 'I must not have much pressure in my life and when I am under a lot of pressure, I can't stand it'), then a core rational philosophy needs be constructed to challenge it in every situation that is operative (e.g. 'I don't want too much pressure in my life, but there is no reason why this must not happen. I can learn to tolerate pressure and thereby improve my coping abilities'). Remember that a core rational philosophy evolves through experimentation in real-life situations and is not instantly formed in the artificial environment of the counsellor's office.

5. Help your clients to understand how they perpetuate their core irrational beliefs.

There are three main ways in which clients perpetuate their core irrational beliefs:

(a) Maintenance of core irrational beliefs

This refers to ways of thinking and behaving that perpetuate core beliefs, e.g. a person who sees himself as boring puts up with jokes from others that talking to him is a good cure for their insomnia; also he takes on the role of 'Mr Boring' in his interactions with others.

(b) Avoidance of core irrational beliefs.

This refers to the cognitive, behavioural and emotional strategies that individuals use to avoid activating core beliefs and the painful feelings associated with them, e.g. a woman steers the conversation away from talk of rejection and loneliness to avoid triggering her self-image as unlovable. This strategy does not work in the long term. For example, through the act of avoidance, the client reminds herself that she is still unlovable.

(c) Compensation for core irrational beliefs.

This refers to behaviours that clients engage in which seem to contradict their core beliefs, e.g. a man who sees himself as incompetent takes on many tasks to prove his competence but this strategy backfires as he fails at some of these tasks and thereby reinforces his belief about himself as a failure.

It is important to help clients not only understand their own particular ways of perpetuating core beliefs but also assist them in developing robust cognitive, emotive and behavioural strategies to halt and then reverse the perpetuation process. For example, in 5(c) above, the client realizes that trying to prove he is competent just continually reminds him that he is incompetent, particularly when he fails to execute tasks successfully. Instead of pursuing this self-defeating strategy any longer, he changes tack and forcefully disputes his 'I must not be incompetent' beliefs and strives for self-acceptance with a strong preference to be task competent. Tasks are now selected on the basis of interest and not to bolster his ego. The client learns eventually to enjoy himself rather than prove himself.

Philosophical v. non-philosophical change

Uprooting rigid and extreme musts and shoulds and their equally uncompromising derivatives of awfulizing, low frustration tolerance, and depreciation of self and others is often referred to in REBT as a profound philosophical change (this kind of change is heavily emphasized in the REBT literature). Philosophical change can occur in specific situations, across situations or become so pervasive that it guides some individuals' daily lives (you do not have to come to therapy to learn REBT philosophy; its primary focus is on educating the wider society in emotional problem-solving, e.g. through self-help literature).

Having said all that, do not coerce or overly influence your clients into believing that philosophical change is the *only* goal on offer in REBT. Obviously when you are discussing REBT with your clients, you will be emphasizing philosophical change as enduring change because REBT views short-term or superficial solutions to emotional problems as generally ineffective. Therefore, persist nondogmatically with philosophically-based change until your clients indicate they are not interested in it or it is beyond their present capabilities, e.g. a client says he wants to learn some relaxation techniques to cope with his panic attacks rather than tackle the panic-inducing belief 'I must not experience panic attacks and it is awful when I do.' Clients can always return to therapy at a later date to pursue a philosophical solution if their non-philosophical one has not helped them in any significant way.

Practical issues may militate against proposing philosophical change, e.g. the emphasis on throughput in the NHS at the possible expense sometimes of tackling core psychological problems, your agency may mandate only a fixed number of sessions. However, you can achieve a lot with relatively few sessions if you learn to be highly problem-focused and thereby 'get on with it'. Having unlimited sessions does not mean that therapy will produce deep-rooted change or that clients will actually want to stay long in therapy. It is important to bear in mind that mean attendance rates in therapy are approximately six sessions (Feltham, 1997).

Assessing progress

Assessment of clients' progress is an important part of therapy as it allows you to check periodically if they are moving towards their goals, have stalled in some way or are falling back after some initial success. It is usually in the working through phase that clients start to realize how deeply entrenched their irrational beliefs are and how many problem areas in their lives these beliefs affect. These and other issues are discussed with John:

Michael: How are you getting on with learning and practising self-acceptance in the face of rejection?

John: That book on self-acceptance you recommended is teaching me not to label myself in any way no matter what happens to me. It is a very different way of looking at yourself. Judge the behaviour, never yourself. I like the idea a lot, so it's helping me to socialize with more women down the pub, at work and in other places.

Michael: Have you asked a woman out yet?

John: No. That's still the hard part.

Michael: Because ... ?

John: Because the old irrational ideas are still there.

Michael: And they're likely to stay there unless you put yourself in the firing line and start getting some rejections.

John: Don't you mean a woman saying 'yes' when I ask her out?

Michael: No, I don't mean that. How are you going to make self-acceptance part of your outlook on life if you avoid getting rejected? If you asked a woman out and she said 'yes' it wouldn't teach you very much. Do you know why?

John: Because I wouldn't have challenged my irrational belief. However, I would feel better about myself because she was interested in me.

Michael: That's right. Your irrational belief would just be put on hold and you would temporarily believe that you were lovable.

John: Temporarily. I agree with that.

Michael: And what would happen if she dumped you a few weeks later?

John: I'd see myself as unlovable yet again. But what if she didn't dump me? Surely that would help me.

Michael: Okay, think it through then. How would it help you?

John: Well, I'd have a woman in my life which is much better than not having one in your life. My belief about being unlovable would disappear as long as ... (voice trails off).

Michael: As long as what?

John: Oh dear, I've fallen into my self-made trap again. As long as I have a woman in my life.

Michael: You keep on making your self-worth conditional whereas you need to make it unconditional if you want to have an enduring solution to your problems.

John: Okay, I get the point: I'll get some rejections before the next session. But surely you don't expect me to put up with rejection for the rest of my life? Is that all you are offering me?

Michael: Of course not. If you learn to take rejection in your stride and thereby not get disturbed about it, what then?

John: Well, obviously I'll get a fair number of rejections but it's more likely some women will go out with me eventually. I'll be able to create more opportunities for myself than I've ever had in my life.

Michael: Exactly. Now in order to really believe in your new rational belief which was ... ?

John: 'I'm not immune from rejection and I can accept myself irrespective of how others see or treat me.'

Michael: I recommend that you say that belief to yourself with force and vigour many times every day so you get it deeply embedded in your head and at the same time keep on hammering away at that irrational belief of yours. You've had that belief for a long time so you won't get rid of it overnight.

John: Tell me about it.

Michael: I know that's not what you mean but let's look at some of the mechanisms that keep irrational beliefs alive, so to speak. These beliefs are maintained over the long term because people act and think in ways that confirm them. For example, a person who thinks he is weak and needy will cling to others, thereby confirming his self-image. Can you think of an example in your case?

John: Well, I suppose I looked for signs from women that they didn't want me, so if I fancied a woman I would be on the look-out for the slightest signs of rejection, like glancing away when she was talking to me, and that would confirm I was unlovable.

Michael: And people don't want to have their irrational beliefs activated or brought face-to-face with them, so they avoid situations that might trigger these beliefs and the unpleasant feelings associated with them such as depression.

John: Like asking women out and getting rejected.

Michael: Exactly.

John: It all makes a lot of sense.

Michael: These beliefs have such a powerful influence on our lives, so the need is for forceful and persistent action against them; hence the importance of homework tasks. If you do them successfully, you can become your own problem-solver while still in therapy and well beyond it as well.

John: Steady on, I haven't reached that stage yet. I still need your help. I haven't been rejected yet! I don't know how I'm going to cope with that.

Michael: Get the rejections and we'll soon know.

Over the next few sessions, John 'collected' several rejections and was able to feel less depressed in the face of them by repeatedly going over his emerging rational beliefs: rejection happens but it does not have to lead to self-depreciation unless he evaluates it in this way. A new problem appeared in the form of low frustration tolerance (LFT): the intense physical and psychological discomfort he experienced prior to, during and after he had been turned down, 'I feel bloody terrible. It's so gut-wrenching putting myself through all of this'. We developed a new belief to counter his LFT and thereby habituate himself to these 'gut-wrenching' encounters: 'If I have to, I'm going to put up with this until hell freezes over. I'm not giving up!'

However, at times, John did get despondent about how hard change was actually proving to be in the real world away from the counsellor's office. To maintain his motivation for change, we used inaction v. action imagery (see 'Imagery tasks' in Chapter 4, p. 64) where action imagery led to a different and much desired way of life whereas inaction imagery represented the 'old' life John desperately wanted to get away from. This exercise became John's primary imaginal means of 'spurring myself on'.

As John was carrying out his programme of change, he began to experience the first glimmerings of emotional insight (i.e. beginning to feel the force of his new rational beliefs in his gut) when he said that asking women out was no longer 'a dreaded experience. Actually, it's not much of a big deal after all.' When he asked one woman out he said, 'she replied "I'll think about it" and I shot back with "Well, don't take too long about it then!" I really surprised myself by saying that.' Along with this breakthrough, John pondered on how to deal with other problems in his life and if they were connected in some way:

John: When I first came to see you I mentioned things I was not getting on with like going down the gym, losing weight and changing my job. I'm doing the first two now and thinking about the job change. I used to think these were all separate problems but I'm not so sure now.

Michael: Is there a theme or belief that connects these problems?

John: I suppose why bother losing weight, getting fit or having a more interesting job when I haven't got a woman in my life.

Michael: Because not having a woman means ... ?

John: I know I said 'unlovable' before but I'm sure it's deeper than that. You see, I also need people to like me. I have great trouble in saying 'no' to people in case they won't like me or reject me.

Michael: So do you think these different problems are linked to a central theme or issue?

John: I'm convinced of it.

Michael: If I was to write all those problems on the whiteboard and had arrows coming from each one, what would be the central point on which they would converge?

John: Hmm. I think it would be worthlessness. Unpleasant to say so, but I think that's the root of it.

Michael: How would the idea of worthlessness be fitted into an irrational belief?

John: Something like 'I must have love and approval from others in order to prove I'm not worthless.'

Michael: How could you test out or observe that this core belief might be operating in other areas of your life as well?

John: I could do a homework task that involves saying 'no' to people when I don't want to do what they ask. A friend of mine, for example, is always asking me for lifts. He thinks I'm a taxi service. I'm sure doing that will help to drag out whatever the core belief is.

Michael: Good. I'll look forward to the feedback. One last question: what's happening with that woman who said she'll get back to you?

John: I got fed up with waiting and asked someone else out. I've been out with Mary now three times. So far, so good.

Michael: Splendid news!

John: You were right about tolerating rejection first. I certainly wouldn't be devastated now if things didn't work out with Mary.

Obstacles to the working through phase

Because working through consumes more time than any other phase of RE[B]T, and also because it requires hard work and responsibility of the client, this segment of the RE[B]T process is filled with potential roadblocks for the therapist and client (Grieger and Boyd, 1980, p. 175).

In this section, we will focus only on client roadblocks. These include the following.

1. Low frustration tolerance

We have discussed LFT already, so just to recap that clients can easily disturb themselves over the hard work required of them to move from intellectual to emotional insight into their problems. Examples of LFT beliefs can include 'I didn't think I'd have to work this hard. I can't stand it!' and 'I'm fed up with these setbacks. I might as well throw the towel in right now.' You will need to encourage your clients to develop a philosophy of effort to cope successfully with the struggle ahead.

2. Cognitive-emotive dissonance

This occurs when clients say they feel 'strange' or 'unnatural' as they work towards strengthening their emerging rational beliefs while still strongly experiencing the 'pull' of their long-standing self defeating thoughts, feelings and behaviours. This dissonant state created by the clash or tension between old and new ways of problem-solving often leads some clients to terminate therapy in order to feel 'natural again'. An example of cognitive-emotive dissonance is the 'I won't be me' syndrome:

Client: It feels very strange not getting angry so often. I'm glad of course but that doesn't take away the strangeness of it.

Therapist: What's so strange about it?

Client: Well, I know it sounds silly but my anger was part of me, if you know what I mean, my sense of who I was. Now there just seems to be a void in me. It feels very strange.

Therapist: Maybe the void is there because you defined yourself too narrowly on the basis of your anger. You are the same person but you get angry less often now. Moving from one self-image to another usually requires a lot of persistence in tolerating these strange feelings until they fade. How do you think you will see yourself in six months, for example, if you put up with this strangeness?

Client: Well, as I want to stop being so angry for all the health benefits we've discussed, I expect six months down the line these new thoughts and feelings will feel more natural to me.

Therapist: And the old angry self, how will you view that?

Client: I suppose that will seem rather strange and distant. As I get further and further away from the old me, I might have trouble recognizing me. Going back to the old me would then seem very strange indeed.

Therapist: So if you want to achieve these new feelings, what will you need to do?

Client: Tolerate these strange feelings I'm experiencing and see them as a natural part of the change process. I'm sure that will help me to get through it more quickly.

Therapist: Exactly. That's the way it usually works.

3. Failing to establish a coping criterion

Some clients may want to discuss new problems in each session before any real progress has been made on the old problems examined in previous sessions. Such a lack of continuity in working through problems may result in the fragmentation of therapy as clients continually 'hop' between problems and thereby fail to tackle any of them successfully. Therefore it is important for you to underscore the need to establish a coping criterion for each problem, i.e. a method of assessing when clients have reached the stage of managing their problems rather than mastering them. A coping criterion helps clients and therapists to determine the right time to switch their clinical focus from one problem to another.

However, if circumstances warrant it, you should be flexible and switch to another problem before a coping criterion is attained on the previous one, e.g. a crisis in the client's life; another issue on your client's problem list is deemed to be of greater clinical importance than the one initially selected. Once the switch has been made, ensure that a coping criterion is reached on this problem before another one is discussed.

4. Pseudo-rationality (Neenan and Dryden, 1996)

This is where some clients, usually a minority, project a false or pretended acceptance of REBT's philosophy of living. They are usually erudite in the theory and practice of REBT and provide the 'correct' answers to the questions you ask. Yet this REBT knowledge is not actually put into daily practice and thereby emotional insight is not realized, i.e. rational principles remain in the client's head instead of being acted upon. Clients who display pseudo-rationality may genuinely believe that intellectual insight alone is sufficient to effect therapeutic change or they may adhere to a philosophy of low frustration tolerance and therefore are reluctant to work hard in and out of therapy. In each case, challenging and changing these attitudes will help these clients to internalize the REBT view of genuine rationality.

5. Fear of mediocrity (Grieger and Boyd, 1980)

Clients with perfectionist traits are often reluctant to surrender their rigid musts and shoulds because they believe these are the basis of their motivation and success in life, e.g. 'If I stop driving myself in this way, my standards will plummet and my success will vanish.' In short, giving up musts and shoulds inevitably leads to mediocrity – what perfectionists dread. It is important to show these clients that introducing flexibility into their thinking about motivation and success does not lead to demotivation and failure; rather it allows them to avoid becoming overly disturbed when standards are not always achieved or success proves temporarily elusive. From a pragmatic viewpoint, the time wasted on emotional disturbance can be more usefully channelled towards problem-solving or engaging in enjoyable activities (perfectionists often pursue achievement to such an extent that little time is left for anything else).

Relapse prevention

Originally applied to the field of substance abuse (Marlatt and Gordon, 1985), the concept is now widely used as part of many therapy approaches. Relapse prevention helps clients to identify those situations (e.g. negative emotional states, interpersonal strife) that could trigger a relapse into their emotional and behavioural difficulties and teaches them coping strategies to deal successfully with these situations. As Beck *et al.* (1993, p. 11) point out: 'Individuals faced with high-risk situations must respond with coping responses. Those who have effective coping responses develop increased self-efficacy, resulting in a decreased probability of relapse.' Obviously, relapse prevention in REBT will be based upon the skills clients have learnt in therapy with you. It is important to build in these coping skills to your treatment plan as 'outcome is increasingly measured not only by treatment success but by relapse prevention' (Padesky and Greenberger, 1995, p. 70).

It is important to teach your clients the difference between a lapse and a relapse: the former state can be seen as a stumble (e.g. one drink) while the latter state involves a collapse (e.g. drunk for the whole weekend). Post-therapy lapses are common but need to be dealt with by clients in order for them to regain self-control and thereby 'halt the slide' into a relapse. Some of your clients may express irritation that relapse prevention is even being discussed because this injects into therapy a pessimistic note, e.g. 'What's the point of working hard in therapy, as you keep on urging me to do, when what you're really saying is it's all going to fall apart anyway when I leave therapy?'

Given REBT's view on our seemingly limitless ability to disturb ourselves about anything in our lives, relapse prevention would seem a realistic strategy to pursue. However, the term 'prevention' seems to offer more than it can probably deliver as it suggests we can stop a full-blown recurrence(s) of the original problem. Maybe the term 'relapse reduction' better describes the post-therapy prognosis of fallible human beings.

Criteria to decide if the working through process has been successful

If the working through phase of therapy has been successful, your clients should be close to termination of therapy because they have:

1. internalized a rational philosophy of living and thereby have made reductions in the frequency, duration and intensity of their presenting emotional problems;
2. successfully applied REBT to their presenting problems as well as other problem areas in their lives;
3. identified, challenged and changed core irrational beliefs;
4. developed confidence and competence acting as self-therapists;
5. agreed with you that termination is near because the evidence points in that direction (i.e. persistent hard work has paid off).

However, the reality is that probably only a few clients will meet the above criteria for termination. Others, for example, will terminate as soon as they experience symptomatic rather than philosophical relief from their problems; or focus on only challenging and changing their situation-specific irrational beliefs, thereby limiting the generalizability of these gains. You can present a rationale to your clients to stay longer in therapy in order to embrace wider philosophical change and thereby make themselves generally less emotionally disturbable but, of course, the final decision regarding termination rests with your clients. You can suggest follow-up appointments to monitor their progress and they can contact you again if they encounter emotional problems they cannot tackle themselves.

Summary of John's progress

John was very surprised by how much progress he had made in two and a half months of therapy. With regard to his presenting problems, he had experienced rejections and learnt how to cope with them without emotional disturbance and self-depreciation. He was learning to embrace self-acceptance and therefore was not judging himself on the basis of his behaviour or how others treated or saw him. He was also looking for another job with better career prospects. Uncovering the core belief of worthlessness was, John declared, 'the heart of the matter and touched almost every area of my life'. He was able to reduce his approval needs and start saying 'no' to those friends who he thought took advantage of him. This action, he said, 'quickly separated real friends from those who saw me as a soft touch'.

His relationship with Mary was going strong but he reminded himself that she could leave him for someone else and that would be 'too bad and nothing else'. Even more revolutionary for John was the idea that *he* might leave the relationship if he was dissatisfied with it – 'When I think things like that, I can hardly believe it's me. Just three months ago those sort of thoughts would never have occurred to me. I wouldn't have dared think them. If a woman showed any interest in me that was enough.' He continued to lose weight and visit the gym twice weekly.

It was not all success, however. John experienced periods of depression because of the lost opportunities and time wasted in his life: 'Why didn't I deal with these problems years ago? I've lost all those years. I should have sorted things out long ago.' John realized that the REBT approach would be to accept the grim reality of those 'lost years' and not 'lose' any more time through depression but, instead, enjoy his new-found happiness: 'I can see the sense in that view but I'm not really convinced by it yet. I haven't reached emotional insight into this problem.' Reaching emotional insight would be part of John's struggle as a self-therapist.

In this book so far, we have looked at REBT from assessment to near termination. In the next and final chapter, we discuss the obstacles that clients and therapists encounter during the beginning, middle and ending stages of REBT.

Chapter 6
Common Obstacles to Progress in REBT

In this chapter, we discuss common obstacles to progress that clients and therapists present during the beginning, middle and ending stages of REBT; and suggest ways of tackling these problems in order to promote client insight and change.

The beginning phase

This phase is characterized by socializing clients into REBT, building a therapeutic alliance, establishing an early problem-solving focus, teaching the ABC model and negotiating the initial homework tasks. As your clients probably have no knowledge of therapy in general and REBT in particular, your responsibility for overseeing the conduct of therapy in the early stages will be especially greater. We first focus upon therapist obstacles to effecting progress in therapy.

Not exploring clients' anticipations and preferences for counselling

You might automatically assume that providing clients with rapid relief from their emotional problems is the main order of therapeutic business and therefore spending time on discovering clients' views on counselling holds up the momentum of therapy. Also, you may believe that exploring such issues is largely irrelevant because no matter what views clients express they are still going to be taught the ABCs of REBT. You think that appearing authoritative and confident is what really counts in clients' eyes and therefore they will quickly 'get the hang of' REBT.

However, this 'one size fits all' approach to therapy is hardly conducive to developing a therapeutic alliance. By discovering clients' anticipations of therapy, important misconceptions that may arise can be corrected (e.g. 'Therapy will get rid of my problems'; 'You talk, I listen and that's how I get better'), thereby reducing the potential for resistance when therapy unfolds in a manner they did not envisage. Encouraging clients to express their preferences for a particular therapeutic relationship helps 'to establish and maintain an appropriately bonded relationship that will encourage each individual client to implement his or her goal-directed therapeutic tasks' (Golden and Dryden, 1986, pp. 368–9). Such idiosyncratic preferences might include a formal, no-nonsense relationship based on the therapist's expertise or a relaxed, informal one with the therapist seen as a confidant. The point of gathering such information is to create a client-friendly environment which encourages them to address their problems within the ABC model – the manner in which this is done is more important than the speed with which it is carried out.

Discussing the past instead of examining the present

REBT is largely an ahistorical approach to emotional problem-solving by focusing on how clients are maintaining their problems rather than how they were acquired (see Chapter 2 for circumstances when your clinical focus should be directed towards the past, pp. 34–6). If you undertake a lengthy historical examination of your clients' problems you may create the impression that the past and not the present is the true focus of therapy and where the 'answer' lies. As Bond (1998, p. 84) observes: 'variables that caused current psychological problems cannot be changed because they occurred in the unalterable past. However, the present variables that maintain these problems can be modified and this is, of course, the goal of psychotherapy.'

While not diminishing the adverse impact on present functioning of past unpleasant events, REBT argues that the real insight into these past events is the irrational and self-defeating beliefs individuals constructed from them and carried forward into the present. You can help your clients to identify, challenge and change these beliefs 'so that tomorrow's existence can be better than yesterday's. In a sense, the person each day chooses to either hold onto disturbed beliefs or to give them up' (Grieger and Boyd, 1980, pp. 76–7).

Failing to pinpoint unhealthy negative emotions for change

As discussed in Chapter 1, REBT divides negative emotions into unhealthy and healthy states with their cognitive correlates of, respectively, demands and preferences. For example, guilt and shame are underpinned by rigid and extreme musts and shoulds while their healthy alternatives of remorse and disappointment are based on preferences and desires. Problems start when you (a) fail to clarify which emotions clients are referring to when they use such terms as 'bad', 'upset', 'down' or 'pissed off' and (b) do not point out the important differences between terms when clients use them interchangeably such as 'depression' and 'sadness'. Unless this confusion is sorted out, you may end up pathologizing healthy negative emotions (e.g. 'upset' turns out to be disappointment) and teaching clients that sadness is as much to be avoided as depression rather than an adaptive response to grim circumstances.

In order to reduce or avoid misunderstandings in describing their feelings and the ones they wish to change, your clients can be encouraged to adopt REBT's emotional vocabulary. Alternatively, clients can use their own feeling language to distinguish between disturbed and nondisturbed affective states, e.g. 'I want to stop losing it [anger] all the time and instead just get pissed off [annoyed] now and again.'

Failing to detect and deal with meta-emotional problems

When assessing clients, primary emotional problems (e.g. anxiety, hurt) it is important to be alert to the possible presence of meta- or secondary emotional problems (e.g. shame about feeling anxious; anger about feeling hurt) that can distract your clients from focusing on their primary problems. If these meta-emotional problems are not detected and dealt with, you may be discussing the cognitive dynamics of anxiety while your client is preoccupied with his 'weakness' for not being able to deal with the problem himself. In order to minimize meta-emotional interference, probe for the presence of secondary problems when clients have pinpointed their primary ones and investigate when clients are not making the expected progress on their primary problems.

The big picture trap

This occurs when therapists 'insist on obtaining a total picture of the client's past, present and future before beginning an intervention program ... obtaining a perfectly complete picture is neither necessary nor advisable' (Grieger and Boyd, 1980, p. 77). Some clients may have left therapy before the 'big picture' emerges, frustrated by the lack of action in tackling their problems because you focused excessively or exclusively on collecting background data. The ABC model offers a rapid way of understanding clients' presenting problems, thereby allowing early problem-solving to begin. For example, a woman who says she still feels deeply hurt by her husband's unfaithfulness five years ago is shown that her hurt is maintained by the belief 'My husband absolutely shouldn't have betrayed my love for him by sleeping with that woman but because he did, I'll never get over it.' Remember that you do not need an extensive life history to uncover such ideas; if you are still keen on seeing the 'big picture' it will probably emerge as therapy unfolds.

Not establishing clearly the B–C connection

If your clients are to understand and agree with the principle and practice of emotional responsibility (i.e. that they largely disturb themselves about adverse life events), then it is vital you show them the instrumental role their irrational beliefs play in maintaining their unhealthy negative emotions. Unfortunately, some of you may pay only cursory or unemphatic attention to teaching the B–C connection and thereby your clients can be understandably confused or defensive when you start challenging their irrational thinking. Attenuating A–C thinking (i.e. other people or events create our emotional problems) and strengthening B–C thinking (i.e. our emotional problems are largely self-induced) needs your constant attention throughout therapy; so remember your own B–C connection: Be Careful that you do not minimize or 'undersell' the central importance of the belief–feeling link.

Client obstacles

Some clients' wariness about committing themselves to REBT stems from misconceptions they hold about its theory and practice. Some of these misconceptions include the following.

1. REBT is a form of brainwashing

Leaving aside clients' erroneous assumptions that they will have no control over their thinking, the brainwashing rumour is that you will 'implant' your viewpoint in clients' minds and they will leave therapy as REBT clones. What REBT actually attempts is encouraging clients to subject their self-defeating beliefs (e.g. 'I can't be happy without a woman in my life') to logical, realistic and pragmatic examination and applies these same criteria to their emerging rational beliefs (e.g. 'I can be happy without a woman in my life though I'd rather be in a relationship'). Ellis (1983) has long argued that scepticism towards all things in life, including REBT, is an important feature of mental health. Therefore, REBTers work towards helping clients to leave therapy more independently minded than when they entered it.

A final point is the way some clients confuse force and energy in the disputing process with indoctrination. Such vigorous disputing has been found to be effective and rapid in removing disturbance-producing ideas, but clients can feel initially overwhelmed by this approach. Hence their suspicions about 'being brainwashed'. Such suspicions can be allayed by you explaining the rationale for such methods.

2. REBT cares nothing for people's feelings

This criticism contends that REBT advocates a purely cognitive approach to understanding ourselves, others and the world; people's emotional reactions are considered irrelevant in this approach. Negative connotations associated with the word 'rational' conjure up images of cold, logical individuals analysing their problems and viewing others with icy detachment. However, this is a caricature of REBT and not its actual practice. Though REBT is primarily a cognitively orientated approach to emotional problem-solving, it does employ other senses or modalities to effect therapeutic change. As we discussed in Chapter 1, thinking, feeling and behaving are interactive and interdependent processes, but in REBT feelings and behaviours are used in the service of promoting changes in our thoughts.

Clients' emotions are almost always at the centre of therapeutic attention as you seek the most efficient way to replace their unhealthy negative emotions (e.g. depression) with healthy negative emotions (e.g. sadness). The most efficient means of emotional change, as far as REBT is concerned, is multimodal disputing of clients' disturbance-producing ideas in order to help them achieve a rational and emotionally stable outlook. The word 'rational' has no sinister meaning, but simply refers to whatever constructive means will help clients attain their goals and live happier and longer lives (for further discussion of misconceptions about REBT see Dryden, Gordon and Neenan, 1997).

Blaming others

Some clients enter therapy with the firm belief that others cause their problems and therefore these others have to change before they can. While agreeing that others may significantly contribute to their problems, you will need to shift the focus away from these others and on to your clients if therapeutic progress is to occur. For example:

Client: He makes me so angry. He won't get a job, sits around the house all day, won't lift a finger to do any housework. Expects me to do it all when I come in from work. He's no husband to me.

Therapist: Why do you put up with it?

Client: I don't. I'm always having a go at him.

Therapist: But nothing changes. Why do you suppose that is?

Client: He doesn't take me seriously.

Therapist: Because ... ?

Client: He knows I won't leave him at the end of the day.

Therapist: So your threats are not credible. What prevents you from making then so?

Client: I couldn't bear living on my own. He's better than loneliness.

Therapist: Just for argument's sake, say I was able to help you see that living on your own could be bearable and could be the final option in a range of options you could use to try and change your husband's behaviour, what then?

Client: Well, I suppose if I could believe all that, then my threats would become credible and he might shift his backside.

Therapist: And also the responsibility for your own personal change now lies in your hands rather than your husband's. You are not dependent on him to make you feel better.

Client: It's a very different way of looking at things but I can see the logic in it. I've also got to get off my backside if I want things to change.

In the above dialogue, the client has agreed that change needs to occur in herself first before she can hope to have any impact on her husband's behaviour. As Hauck (1991b, p. 199) points out: 'There are two principles of human interaction: 1) We get the behaviour we tolerate; and 2) if we want to change someone else's behaviour, we must change ours first.' This observation is useful to explain to your clients if they really want to effect change in their lives and stop blaming others for their problems.

The cathartic cure myth (Grieger and Boyd, 1980)

This refers to the release of long-suppressed emotions (e.g. anger, guilt) in the first or initial sessions of therapy and as clients now feel 'cleansed' they conclude that therapy is finished, e.g. 'I feel great. I never suspected it would be so quick.' From the REBT perspective, disturbed emotions have been ventilated but not removed because the ideas that give rise to these emotions have not been examined. Frequently, when clients leave therapy prematurely on a 'high', this proves to be short-lived as these underlying ideas engender further disturbed feelings. Encourage your clients to stay longer in therapy to seek enduring methods of change.

'Change must be easy'

Clients who hold this idea usually subscribe to a philosophy of low frustration tolerance (LFT) and, from their perspective, understandably recoil from REBT's emphasis on hard work and practice to effect constructive change. By exerting only minimal effort in personal problem-solving, they perpetuate their problems and create more discomfort for themselves over the longer term than would be the case if they had pushed themselves to promote change in the short term. You can point out to these clients that 'no pain now means no gain later'. Ellis (1985b, p. 102) advises that 'it is sometimes wise to forcefully bring their LFT to their attention and to insist that unless they deliberately and often court discomfort they have virtually no chance of changing or of benefiting from therapy'. The message to these clients is: make yourselves uncomfortable now in order to feel comfortable in the longer-term.

The middle phase

During this phase, the therapeutic focus is on helping your clients to strengthen their emerging rational beliefs and weaken their powerfully held irrational beliefs. This is achieved by you encouraging your clients to use multimodal methods of disputing in a variety of problematic contexts. It is especially important to be on the lookout for the presence of core irrational beliefs that link your clients' problems. This phase is often referred to as rational emotive behavioural working through (see previous chapter). Therapist blocks encountered in this phase will now be explored.

'Therapist, hold thy tongue!' (Neenan and Dryden, 1996)

While greater use of short didactic presentations of REBT concepts are usually made in the early stages of therapy as clients are socialized into REBT, their frequent use during the middle phase of therapy is contraindicated as this may undermine or impair the development of clients' roles as self-therapists. Clients' ability to think through their problems depends on the amount of lecturing that you do. Too much of it can help turn your clients into passive partners in therapy who parrot REBT tenets rather than active and increasingly independently-minded problem-solvers.

Dryden's (1994b) injunction to 'let your clients' brains take the strain' means a corresponding decrease in your level of verbal activity. Instead of lectures, use Socratic dialogue as much as possible, e.g. 'What are the implications for you if change is based on self-esteem instead of self-acceptance?'; 'How were you able to stay in that situation when only a few weeks ago you would have fled from it?' You cannot do the thinking for clients when they leave therapy, so while they remain with you encourage them to take cognitive control of the change process. This will help to ensure their cognitive wheels are turning and not stopped or slowed down because you would not let them get a word in edgeways.

Not explaining to clients the differences between intellectual and emotional insight

This usually occurs when you believe that intellectual insight alone is sufficient to promote therapeutic change, e.g. 'Once you understand how rational thinking will tackle your anxiety, you will be surprised how quickly you can make progress.' Understanding in one's head the efficacy of rational ideas is often a far remove from putting them into daily practice and encountering the struggle and setbacks of real-life change (emotional insight). Leaving your clients marooned at the level of intellectual insight will mean that therapy slips into a discourse on rational ideas instead of an enactment of them.

In order for your clients to reach emotional insight into their problems, encourage them to undertake and experiment with a wide range of homework tasks (e.g. shame attacking exercises, flooding assignments) in order to internalize a rational outlook – 'I feel it in my gut.' Remember that intellectual insight is usually acquired sitting in your office while emotional insight is gained only by stepping into and staying in fearful or aversive situations that are usually avoided.

When homework tasks are not therapeutically potent

As discussed above, homework is the bridge between intellectual and emotional insight. Some clients may not get far along that bridge or take an inordinately long time to cross it because the tasks you have negotiated with them are insufficiently challenging to effect change. For example, you may agree with your client's 'tiny steps' strategy for overcoming her social anxiety, thereby prolonging it instead of encouraging her to stay in social situations for as long as possible in order to habituate herself to the discomfort involved. The 'tiny steps' approach lacks the therapeutic potency to stimulate constructive change as it actually reinforces the client's low frustration tolerance ideas, e.g. 'I have to go very slowly as I'm afraid of feeling uncomfortable.' Unfortunately, you would be colluding with this anti-therapeutic strategy.

In planning and negotiating homework assignments, it is important for you to consider if the designated tasks will help your clients to come appreciably closer to their goals, but without discouraging them from undertaking these tasks because they appear too difficult to execute, e.g. the client agrees to enter social situations thrice weekly to tackle her anxiety but believes that entering them every day would be beyond her ability at this stage of therapy. Dryden (1995a) calls this principle of homework negotiation 'challenging, but not overwhelming' (see Chapter 4 for discussion of this principle).

Failing to uncover core irrational beliefs

As clients' situation-specific irrational beliefs are uncovered (e.g. 'I must never show any weaknesses in front of my colleagues'; 'I must never let my family down'; 'My friends must see how successful I am') they usually suggest a common theme(s) which coalesces in a core irrational belief which links these problems. With regard to the above examples, the core belief might be 'I must always be strong and successful because if I'm not this proves how utterly weak and pathetic I am.' By working at this fundamental cognitive level you can help your clients achieve profound and enduring change in their lives as many problems are tackled concurrently instead of consecutively.

However, although you may assume that tackling each irrational belief as it is revealed is profound philosophical change of a sort, this is actually a haphazard way of achieving it as it leaves your clients vulnerable to emotional disturbances in problematic contexts that have not been examined. Also, plodding through each problem may give your clients tunnel vision rather than offering them a panorama of their problems by tapping into their rules of living or core philosophies. In order to avoid this limiting therapeutic strategy, ask your clients if they can discern central ideas or themes that recur in each problem which is analysed. If your clients are unable to identify key themes or ideas located in their problems, then suggest to them what they might be and seek feedback in order to confirm, modify or reject your suggestions.

'My disputing isn't working'

Disputing clients' irrational ideas is probably the principal activity of REBTers. The degree of skill, persistence and creativity you show in the disputing process often means the difference between sustained and temporary emotional change. Ellis (1979b, 1985b) emphasizes the role of force and energy in eradicating often deeply rooted musturbatory (musts) ideas. Some therapists, usually novice ones, believe that a few tilts at an irrational belief using standard REBT questions (e.g. 'Where's the evidence you must never make mistakes?') will bring it crashing down and its rational alternative will automatically spring up in its place. More commonly, you can become disillusioned about not making any therapeutic headway when your clients show no signs of surrendering or weakening their irrational ideas. Power struggles can ensue if you become determined to make your clients 'see sense and stop resisting my arguments'.

Disputing is undertaken to persuade your clients of the effectiveness of rational ideas in emotional problem-solving. It is not a power struggle where you *have* to convince your clients of REBT's 'rational correctness'. The standard logical, empirical and pragmatic arguments are only the starting point in the disputing process and not the process itself. Hauck (1980) suggests that your credibility and strength as an REBT therapist is partly due to the ease with which you can employ a wide range of rational arguments to turn the tide in your clients' thinking. Effective disputing involves creativity, humour, risk-taking, persistence, repetition, force and energy in order to make your rational case to your clients. By developing a genuine enthusiasm for analysing argument, disputing becomes more of a pleasure and less of a chore.

Client obstacles

Some of these have already been discussed in the working through phase of therapy (see Chapter 5). Other client blocks include the following.

Employing non-philosophical methods towards achieving philosophical change

During the middle phase of therapy, you should determine the nature of your clients' progress in tackling their emotional problems. REBT's preferred solution (but not always the client's one) is philosophical whereby your clients uproot their 'musturbatory' thinking and replace it with rational preferences and desires. Non-philosophical solutions involve changing distorted negative inferences instead of the underlying irrational ideas from which they derive, effecting behaviourally-based change or altering or avoiding unpleasant activating events rather than confronting them.

Some clients want the enduring benefits of a profound philosophical change in their thinking yet use non-philosophical methods to achieve it. For example, a man who decides his inferences were wrong about his work colleagues' dislike of him fails to focus on the implicit irrational belief that 'They must like me in order for me to accept myself.' The danger here is that his disturbance-inducing idea has been left intact and the client has not learnt any coping strategies if his inferences eventually turn out to be true (a philosophical strategy would be to learn self-acceptance irrespective of how his work colleagues or anyone else views him).

Inferentially-based change, like the other two non-philosophical solutions, has limited generalizability to his other problems because it does not pinpoint the philosophical sources (i.e. rigid musts and shoulds) of his emotional problems and how these are linked, e.g. in the above example, the need for others' approval. Revealing and disputing these underlying ideas provides the most efficient means of tackling his problems rather than challenging his inferences in every problem area he identifies.

This discrepancy between desiring philosophical change but using non-philosophical means to achieve it may arise because your clients, among other reasons, repeat parrot-fashion rational ideas, dispute irrational ideas in a perfunctory way without realizing that consistent and forceful action is really required of them, or want lasting change with little effort. To deal with this problem, you can clearly outline the considerable steps involved in philosophical change and contrast these with your clients' lack of commensurate effort to attain it.

'I didn't think change would be this hard'

Dryden (1990, p. 84) states that it is 'during the middle stage of rational-emotive counselling that clients show most resistance to change'. They may have had an initial surge of progress or optimism in tackling their problems but now have experienced setbacks, faltering progress or the sheer grind of overcoming a long-standing problem. Such obstacles can lead to disillusionment or despair over the realities of change:

Client: I wonder if it's worth going on in therapy.

Therapist: Because ... ?

Client: Well, nothing seems to be going right: one step forward and three steps back. I have to keep pushing myself all the time.

Therapist: How long have you had your drink and drug problems?

Client: About ten years. You know that.

Therapist: How long do you think it will take to overcome them?

Client: I don't know. How long is a piece of string?

Therapist: You've been in therapy now for two months and you have made some progress. If you've spent ten years using drink and drugs to disastrous effect in your life, what's the problem with spending six months or a year learning how to cope without them?

Client: (irritably) I just thought it would be easier than this.

Therapist: Do you mean ten days to clean up ten years?

Client: Yes, something like that.

Therapist: What belief might be behind all this complaining about how hard change is?

Client: 'It shouldn't be this bloody difficult. I'm fucked off with it.' But you knew that.

Therapist: I guessed it was something along those lines. Do you know why change should be hard rather than shouldn't be?

Client: Oh dear. This sounds like another painful lesson I don't want to learn. Go on, tell me why.

Therapist: Because of the sheer magnitude and complexity of the problems you've experienced in the last ten years. It would be nothing short of a miracle if you could sort yourself out in ten days. But you will make the change process much harder than it has to be if you keep on moaning and complaining all the time. Now all this valuable energy you are wasting on moaning could be used ...

Client: ... in working on my problems instead of whining about them. I get pissed off with all my whingeing and whining too.

Therapist: Okay, how about being more of a worker and less of a whinger?

Client: I'll do my best but don't expect me to be happy about it.

Therapist: It's the attitude of coping constructively with frustrations and setbacks that I want you to learn. Happiness doesn't usually come into it.

Client: And if I do learn this attitude, what then?

Therapist: Well, we'll probably see one step forward and only two steps back now.

Client: (mockingly) Great.

REBT hypothesizes that low frustration tolerance (LFT) is probably the major reason why clients terminate therapy when the hard work of change 'kicks in' as they avoid making themselves deliberately uncomfortable in the present in order to feel comfortable in the future. You will need to make explicit your clients' often implicit LFT ideas and forcefully encourage them to dispute these ideas in order to acquire higher frustration tolerance (HFT) which, in turn, will make it more likely they will realize their therapeutic goals.

Avoiding becoming a self-therapist

As counsellor directiveness fades during therapy, there should be a corresponding increase in the lead taken by clients in using the ABCs of self-analysis and change as well as setting and executing homework tasks. However, some of your clients will be reluctant to grasp the nettle of self-responsibility for change. Reasons for this reluctance include: fear of failure in their new role; LFT-related beliefs regarding the additional and more demanding work now involved; this phase heralds the beginning of the end of therapy and some clients do not wish to acknowledge this and, instead, want to prolong therapy by remaining dependent on you; resistance to becoming self-counsellors, as this is perceived by clients as you abdicating your responsibility as their problem-solver. Whatever the reason, you will need to draw out and examine the ideas blocking this necessary shift in therapeutic responsibility; such ideas will be frequently linked to your clients' presenting problems, e.g. 'I can't cope on my own.'

Power struggles

Experienced REBTers usually like to present themselves as authoritative (but not authoritarian) teachers of emotional problem-solving. Some clients will rebel against such teaching and flagrantly 'shoot down' whatever you say or, more subtly, engage in 'yes, but' exchanges which initially agree with your viewpoint but are actually saying 'no', e.g. 'I can see the sense in what you say about risk-taking exercises but they wouldn't really tackle my anxiety.' You may feel that therapy is developing into a power struggle as you and your client struggle for supremacy.

If this is the case, pull out of it as you have nothing to prove to your antagonistic clients. Suggest to them: (1) your ego is not on the line and you will not be unhappy if you 'lose the fight' or they leave therapy; (2) they can play games in therapy if they wish but the consequences are predictable: they will waste time and still be emotionally disturbed at the end of therapy; (3) possible reasons for their need to win: self-depreciation if they do not, they are acting angrily because they perceive they are being told what to do, or they have chronic LFT which leads them to avoid the hard work of change but rise to the enjoyable challenge of 'working' to destabilize therapy. If you leave the decisions about progress in therapy to such clients (e.g. 'Stay or go; it's entirely up you'), you will avoid getting sucked into power struggles or playing games and, surprisingly, you may find that some of these clients will actually 'shape up' when they see your lack of interest in their anti-therapeutic antics.

The ending phase

In this stage of therapy, you and your clients agree to work towards termination by decreasing session frequency or setting a fixed date for the final session. Progress is reviewed and what your clients have learnt from therapy and future challenges as self-therapists are discussed; any termination issues are tackled. Some therapist obstacles in this phase will now be examined.

Taking too much credit for your clients' progress

As therapy moves towards termination, it is important for you to attribute the majority of clients' progress to them and not to yourself, even if some clients insist on it, e.g. 'It may seem like I did the work but you, not me, went into those anxious situations day after day. Your tremendous effort brought about these changes in your life. I showed you the way but you followed it.' This kind of summary puts the locus of control and change within clients and is often a powerful stimulus for them to maintain their gains after termination. Some therapists may be reluctant to give too much credit to their clients for making progress, thereby diminishing their own contributions to it; instead, these therapists convey to their clients how 'dazzling' they were in orchestrating the change process, e.g. 'Once I had uncovered that core belief of yours and got you to see how many problems it caused in your life, there wasn't much for you to do after that. Therapy took care of itself.' Comments like these relegate clients to the sidelines of therapy. Such self-adoration is likely to communicate to clients that 'you can't do it without me' and, if believed by them, may increase their chances of backsliding once therapy has finished.

Therapists who feed their vanity as the omnipotent forces of change in clients' lives usually have considerable ego problems, e.g. 'I need clients to see and acknowledge how great I am in getting them better.' By challenging and changing such beliefs, these therapists can remove their egos from therapy and focus their clinical attention in the right direction – making sure that their clients are equipped to leave therapy as emotional problem-solvers. The real satisfaction for the REBT therapist is not blowing her own trumpet but seeing her clients acquire a rational outlook that can help to guide them for the rest of their lives.

Unwilling to terminate therapy

REBT therapists do not usually attempt to keep their clients in therapy once they have shown their skill as self-therapists. To do so might be counterproductive as clients begin to doubt their hard-won problem-solving abilities, e.g. 'I feel ready to leave and try it on my own but he keeps saying another couple of sessions. Is there something he isn't telling me? Maybe I'm not ready yet.' Clients' doubts about acting as self-therapists would be unwarranted in this context as the real problem lies with their therapist: namely, that he needs continued evidence of clients' progress in order to prove to himself that he is a competent clinician.

Clients are therefore held back from leaving therapy because of the therapist's needs. Obviously this therapist's self-defeating and potentially client-harming ideas need to be challenged and changed. Maybe then he can see that clinical competence not only helps clients to develop effective problem-solving skills but also encourages them when the time is right to strike out on their own.

'It's not time to go: I haven't done proper REBT yet'

The therapist's preferred client goals for change are often more far-reaching than the client's. The ideal REBT goal is for clients to remove or minimize their rigid and extreme thinking and strive for unconditional self-acceptance as fallible human beings. Some or even many clients will not be interested in these goals and only want to achieve their more limited agendas such as finding symptom relief from excessive anxiety or ventilating their worries but without accompanying action to tackle them. When these aims are achieved they will want to leave therapy. Some REBTers may become alarmed by this suggestion because they believe they are short-changing their clients if they do not embrace philosophical change or 'correct' REBT. The clients, however, have reached a plateau of change and do not want to be prodded, pushed or persuaded to ascend to the peak of 'what could be'. Because these therapists are probably rigidly interpreting REBT's preferred practice they are more likely to view themselves as failures if these clients only want non-philosophical change. Hence their pleas for these clients to stay in therapy.

Such therapists would be wise to remember that the philosophical solution to emotional problem-solving is offered to clients and not imposed upon them. It is not a sign of therapist failure if some clients choose not to pursue this solution, but a salutary reminder to presumptuous therapists that REBT is not the panacea for all psychological ills and people can still be happy and productive if they hold on to some rigid musts and absolute shoulds. That the degree of change is to clients' satisfaction, though maybe not containing much depth to it, should be the source of therapists' congratulations rather than despair over their clients' short-sightedness in settling for superficial solutions. In the final analysis, REBT's philosophical solution to emotional disturbance, though much discussed and advocated in the REBT field, remains only an hypothesis and has not yet received empirical support in the psychotherapy research literature (see Bond and Dryden, 1996).

Client obstacles

These often involve clients' fears about coping on their own and terminating what might have been a close relationship.

In Chapter 3 we discussed how to conduct multimodal (cognitive, behavioural, emotive, imaginal) disputing of clients' irrational beliefs with particular emphasis on structured cognitive disputing whereby irrational and rational beliefs are examined concurrently. In Chapter 4 we showed you how to devise and negotiate homework or real-life tasks with your clients which enable them to weaken their adherence to irrational beliefs and strengthen their commitment to emerging rational beliefs.

In Chapter 5 we turned our attention to the working through phase which requires hard work from clients to move their rational ideas from their heads and into their guts, and then to keep them there through sustained, often lifelong, effort.

Finally, in Chapter 6, we discussed how you can identify and tackle both your clients' and your own obstacles to constructive change as therapy moves through its stages of beginning, middle and end.

Ultimately, REBT seeks to be of relatively short duration in its counselling, focuses on and eradicates or modifies core disturbance-producing, and strives to have an enduring impact on clients' lives. Few therapies seek to be so ambitious.

'It's not time to leave yet'

Instead of prematurely terminating therapy, some clients will want to stay in therapy as long as possible. This need for long-term therapy will often prove clinically counterproductive as any progress already made may begin to erode as these clients look for ways to delay striking out on their own. This may occur because they believe, among other reasons, they must feel completely confident about coping on their own, conditions in their lives have to be perfect before leaving therapy or their problems should be completely resolved first.

If severing the therapeutic relationship 'does become a major issue, then the client is not ready to terminate, for this is an indication that the client relies on the therapist to fulfil some perceived need – perhaps approval, reassurance, or freedom from responsibility' (Wessler and Wessler, 1980, p. 182). In the above examples, you can challenge these termination-blocking ideas by stating: increased rather than complete confidence about problem-solving is more likely to occur once clients have left therapy rather than remaining indefinitely within it; creating 'perfect' or, more realistically, favourable conditions in one's life requires sustained hard work and determination that lingering in therapy will not provide – such clients are distracting themselves with utopian fantasies instead of focusing upon practical realities; managing one's problems instead of completely resolving them is the benchmark for decisions about terminating therapy. Frequently underlying this reluctance to leave therapy is the fear of failing as a self-therapist.

'I can't sort out my problems on my own'

REBT's ultimate aim is to help clients become effective problem-solvers. For some clients, this new role will bring a feeling of exhilaration, but for others it may fill them with a sense of dread particularly if they have experienced a relapse prior to termination. The reactivation of clients' presenting symptoms so close to termination 'is not a phenomenon unique to RE[B]T, nor is it anything to become alarmed about. The most useful thing for the therapist to do when these fears arise is to simply help clients discover what they are telling themselves to become upset and to work these notions through' (Grieger and Boyd, 1980, p. 190):

Client: I was going great guns with my progress and then it all fell apart over the weekend. How can I leave therapy now? I'm not ready.

Therapist: First of all, what happened at the weekend?

Client: I had a bad panic attack in the supermarket. I had to leave immediately and come straight home.

Therapist: It's good that you got yourself home. Now what were you telling yourself to make yourself leave the supermarket whereas you usually stay in the supermarket and wait until the symptoms subside?

Client: Well, I suppose this time I told myself I couldn't stand the panic. I'm not sure why it happened. Maybe because I hadn't slept the previous night and I had a row with my husband before I went to the supermarket. I felt jittery and angry on my way there.

Therapist: I'm sure these things didn't help but, more importantly, what are you now going to do about your setback?

Client: Go into the supermarket today and if the panic hits, then just stay with it until it blows itself out.

Therapist: Just today?

Client: No. Every day for the next week.

Therapist: Even twice a day to prove ... ?

Client: That I don't have to be in complete control of the problem.

Therapist: Exactly. Now you got yourself quite upset over this setback – are there any irrational ideas lurking in the background about your progress as a self-therapist?

Client: I didn't think so until last weekend, but now I realize because I was making such good progress, then it must always be like that.

Therapist: And the must wasn't met last weekend so ... ?

Client: So I thought that all my progress had been wiped out and I would never make any more. It was truly awful at the time.

Therapist: And now after rational reflection?

Client: I overreacted to a setback. Progress is never so smooth and setbacks will occur. I will deal with them constructively and without despair as you once said.

Therapist: Good. Do you still think you're not ready to leave therapy?

Client: No. I am ready to leave. I need to keep on reminding myself that as a self-therapist I will have my ups and downs. I'm feeling more optimistic and realistic now.

In the above extract, the setback near the end of therapy is not the problem but the client's awfulizing about it; namely, that all her therapeutic

gains have been wiped out because of her failure on this withstand her panic symptoms. Therefore she concludes leave therapy now. Another block to independent problem-unrealistic idea that progress must be uninterrupted. Th discussed and realistic conclusions drawn about the real na self-therapist.

Struggling with ambivalence

Some clients are eager to leave therapy and stand on th they feel sad about terminating what they consider to ha tant relationship in their lives. They may believe that fee negative emotion) is a sign of weakness or 'not being ra to suppress this feeling in the last session while stru brave face. It is important that you are alert to clues wrestling with these feelings and tease out the poss lying behind them, e.g. 'I've got to be upbeat and session because if I show any sadness this will n practising REBT.'

Obviously the above example shows that this clie learning to undertake as sadness is not a feeli suppress. This misunderstanding can be tackled w discussion and some homework tasks (e.g. fur which can be reviewed in the follow-up appoi indicates, REBTers keep a problem-solving focus Despite some clients' ambivalence about termi discuss in the final session is clients' progress a primarily pleasant events' (Wessler and Wessler

Summary

In this book, we hope we have provided you rational emotive behaviour therapy. Let us j done.

- In Chapter 1 we explained the role of ri and their extreme derivatives which a emotional disturbance, and contrast producing flexible preferences and wi atives.
- In Chapter 2 we showed you how to of clients' presenting emotional p irrational beliefs largely maintaini why it is important to establish clie

Appendix

For information on REBT training in Britain contact:

Professor Windy Dryden
PACE
Goldsmiths College
New Cross
London SE14 6NW
Tel: 0171 919 7872

Dr Stephen Palmer
Centre for REBT
156 Westcombe Hill
Blackheath
London SE3 7DH
Tel: 0181 293 4114

For further details on REBT training worldwide contact:

Director of Professional Education
Albert Ellis Institute for Rational Emotive Behavior Therapy
45 East 65th Street
New York
NY 10021
USA
Tel: 001 212 535 0822

References

Bard J (1980) Rational-Emotive Therapy in Practice. Champaign, IL: Research Press.

Beck AT, Wright FD, Newman CF, Liese BS (1993) Cognitive Therapy of Substance Abuse. New York: Guilford.

Beck JS (1995) Cognitive Therapy: Basics and Beyond. New York: Guilford.

Bond FW (1998) Using a case formulation to understand and treat a person with generalised anxiety disorder. In Bruch M and Bond FW (eds), Beyond Diagnosis: Case Formulation Approaches in CBT. Chichester: John Wiley & Sons.

Bond FW, Dryden W (1996) Why two, central REBT hypotheses appear untestable. Journal of Rational-Emotive & Cognitive-Behavior Therapy 14(1): 29–40.

Burns DD (1989) The Feeling Good Handbook. New York: William Morrow.

DiGiuseppe R (1989) (audio cassette recording) What Do I Do With My Anger: Hold It In or Let It Out? New York: Albert Ellis Institute for Rational Emotive Behavior Therapy.

DiGiuseppe R (1991) Comprehensive cognitive disputing in RET. In Bernard ME (ed), Using Rational-Emotive Therapy Effectively: A Practitioner's Guide. New York: Plenum.

Dryden W (1990) Rational-Emotive Counselling in Action. London: Sage.

Dryden W (1991a) Reason and Therapeutic Change. London: Whurr.

Dryden W. (1991b) A Dialogue with Albert Ellis: Against Dogma. Buckingham: Open University Press.

Dryden W (1994a) 10 Steps to Positive Living. London: Sheldon Press.

Dryden W (1994b) Progress in Rational Emotive Behaviour Therapy. London: Whurr.

Dryden W (1995a) Facilitating Client Change in Rational Emotive Behaviour Therapy. London: Whurr.

Dryden W (1995b) Brief Rational Emotive Behaviour Therapy. Chichester: John Wiley & Sons.

Dryden W (1999a) Rational Emotive Behaviour Therapy: A Personal Approach. Bicester, Oxford: Winslow Press.

Dryden W (1999b) How to Develop Self-Acceptance. London: Sheldon Press.

Dryden W, DiGiuseppe R (1990) A Primer on Rational-Emotive Therapy. Champaign, IL: Research Press.

Dryden W, Gordon J, Neenan M (1997) What is Rational Emotive Behaviour Therapy? Loughton, Essex: Gale Centre Publications.

Dryden W, Neenan M, Yankura J (1999) Counselling Individuals: A Rational Emotive Behavioural Handbook, 3rd edition. London: Whurr.

Dryden W, Yankura J (1995) Developing Rational Emotive Behavioural Counselling. London: Sage Publications.

Ellis A (1969) A weekend of rational encounter. In Burton A (ed), Encounter: The Theory and Practice of Encounter Groups. San Francisco, CA: Jossey-Bass.

Ellis A (1972) Helping people to get better rather than merely feel better. Rational Living 7 (2): 2–9.

Ellis A (1976) The biological basis of human irrationality. Journal of Individual Psychology 32. 145–68.

Ellis A (1979a) (audio cassette recording) RET and Assertiveness Training. New York: Albert Ellis Institute for Rational Emotive Behavior Therapy.

Ellis A (1979b) The issue of force and energy in behavior change. Journal of Contemporary Psychotherapy 10: 83–97.

Ellis A (1983) The Case Against Religiosity. New York: Albert Ellis Institute for Rational Emotive Behavior Therapy.

Ellis A. (1984) How to Maintain and Enhance Your Rational-Emotive Therapy Gains. New York: Albert Ellis Institute for Rational Emotive Behavior Therapy.

Ellis A (1985a) Expanding the ABCs of rational-emotive therapy. In Mahoney M, Freeman A (eds), Cognition and Psychotherapy. New York: Plenum.

Ellis A (1985b) Overcoming Resistance: Rational-Emotive Therapy with Difficult Clients. New York: Springer.

Ellis A (1986) (audio cassette recording) Unconditionally Accepting Yourself and Others. New York: Albert Ellis Institute for Rational Emotive Behavior Therapy.

Ellis A (1991) The revised ABCs of rational-emotive therapy (RET). Journal of Rational-Emotive & Cognitive-Behavior Therapy, 139–72.

Ellis A (1993) Fundamentals of rational-emotive therapy for the 1990s. In Dryden W, Hill LK (eds), Innovations in Rational-Emotive Therapy. London: Sage.

Ellis A (1994) Reason and Emotion in Psychotherapy, revised and updated. New York: Birch Lane Press.

Ellis A (1997) Postmodern ethics for active-directive counseling and psychotherapy. Journal of Mental Health Counseling 18: 211–25.

Ellis A (1999) Rational emotive behavior therapy and cognitive behavior therapy for elderly people. Journal of Rational-Emotive and Cognitive-Behavior Therapy 17(1): 5–18.

Ellis A, Bernard ME (eds) (1985) The Clinical Applications of Rational-Emotive Therapy. New York: Plenum Press.

Ellis A, Dryden W (1997) The Practice of Rational Emotive Behavior Therapy, 2nd edition. New York: Springer.

Ellis A, Harper R (1975) A New Guide to Rational Living. Englewood Cliffs, NJ: Prentice-Hall.

Ellis A, Knaus WJ (1977) Overcoming Procrastination. New York: Albert Ellis Institute for Rational Emotive Behavior Therapy.

Ellis A, McInerney JF, DiGiuseppe R, Yeager RJ (1988) Rational-Emotive Therapy with Alcoholics and Substance Abusers. New York: Pergamon Press.

Ellis A, MacLaren C (1998) Rational Emotive Behavior Therapy: A Therapist's Guide. San Luis Obispo, CA: Impact Publishers.

Ellis A, Young J, Lockwood G (1987) Cognitive therapy and rational-emotive therapy: a dialogue. Journal of Cognitive Psychotherapy 1(4): 205–55.

Feltham C (1997) Time-Limited Counselling. London: Sage Publications.

Golden WL, Dryden W (1986) Cognitive-behavioural therapies: commonalities, divergences and future developments. In Dryden W, Golden W (eds), Cognitive-Behavioural Approaches to Psychotherapy. London: Harper & Row.

Grieger RM (1991) Keys to effective RET. In Bernard ME (ed), Using Rational-Emotive Therapy Effectively: A Practitioner's Guide. New York: Plenum.

Grieger RM, Boyd J (1980) Rational-Emotive Therapy: A Skills-Based Approach. New York: Van Nostrand Reinhold.

Hauck PA (1966) The neurotic agreement in psychotherapy. Rational Living 1(1): 31–4.

Hauck PA (1980) Brief Counseling with RET. Philadelphia, PA: Westminster Press.

Hauck PA (1991a) Hold Your Head Up High. London: Sheldon Press.

Hauck PA (1991b) RET and the assertive process. In Bernard ME (ed), Using Rational-Emotive Therapy Effectively: A Practitioner's Guide. New York: Plenum.

Lazarus AA (1984) In the Mind's Eye. New York: Guilford Press.

Leahy RL (1998)(book review)Treating anxiety disorders. Journal of Cognitive Psychotherapy 12(4): 350–3.

McMullin RE (1986) Handbook of Cognitive Therapy Techniques. New York: W.W. Norton & Co.

Marlatt GA, Gordon JR (1985) Relapse Prevention: Maintenance Strategies in the Treatment of Addictive Behaviors. New York: Guilford.

Maultsby M (1975) Help Yourself to Happiness. New York: Albert Ellis Institute for Rational Emotive Behavior Therapy.

Maultsby M, Ellis A (1974) Techniques for Using Rational-Emotive Imagery. New York: Albert Ellis Institute for Rational Emotive Behavior Therapy.

Neenan M, Dryden W (1996) Dealing with Difficulties in Rational Emotive Behaviour Therapy. London: Whurr.

Neenan M, Dryden W (1999) Rational Emotive Behaviour Therapy: Advances in Theory and Practice. London: Whurr.

Neenan M, Palmer S (1998) A cognitive-behavioural approach to tackling stress. Counselling, the Journal of the British Association for Counselling 9(4): 315–19.

Padesky CA, Greenberger D (1995) Clinician's Guide to Mind Over Mood. New York: Guilford.

Persons JB (1989) Cognitive Therapy in Practice: A Case Formulation Approach. New York: W.W. Norton.

Scott MJ, Stradling SG, Dryden W (1995) Developing Cognitive-Behavioural Counselling. London: Sage.

Tarnas R (1996) The Passion of the Western Mind. London: Pimlico.

Vesey G, Foulkes P (1990) Dictionary of Philosophy. London: HarperCollins.

Walen S, DiGiuseppe R, Dryden W (1992) A Practitioner's Guide to Rational-Emotive Therapy, 2nd edition. New York: Oxford University Press.

Wessler RA, Wessler RL (1980) The Principles and Practice of Rational-Emotive Therapy. San Francisco, CA: Jossey-Bass.

Yankura J, Dryden W (1994) Albert Ellis. London: Sage Publications.

Young HS (1974) A Rational Counseling Primer. New York: Albert Ellis Institute for Rational Emotive Behavior Therapy.

Index